sabrina soto
home design

a layer-by-layer approach to turning your ideas
into the home of your dreams

by Sabrina Soto

WILEY

John Wiley & Sons, Inc.

Acquisitions Editor
Pam Mourouzis

Copy Editor
Lynn Northrup

Senior Project Editor
Donna Wright

Editorial Manager
Christina Stambaugh

Vice President and Publisher
Cindy Kitchel

Vice President and Executive Publisher
Kathy Nebenhaus

Interior Design
Erin Zeltner

Cover Design
Aram Youssefian

Graphics
Laura Campbell
Ana Carrillo
Brent Savage

Sabrina Soto Home Design: A Layer-by-Layer Approach to Turning Your Ideas into the Home of Your Dreams

Published by John Wiley & Sons, Inc., Hoboken, New Jersey

Published simultaneously in Canada

For general information on our other products and services or to obtain technical support please contact our Customer Care Department within the U.S. at (877) 762-2974, outside the U.S. at (317) 572-3993 or fax (317) 572-4002.

John Wiley & Sons, Inc., also publishes its books in a variety of electronic formats and by print-on-demand. Not all content that is available in standard print versions of this book may appear or be packaged in all book formats. If you have purchased a version of this book that did not include media that is referenced by or accompanies a standard print version, you may request this media by visiting http://booksupport.wiley.com. For more information about Wiley products, visit us at www.wiley.com.

Library of Congress Control Number: 2012933407

ISBN: 978-1-118-10078-3 (pbk)

ISBN: 978-1-118-18230-7; 978-1-118-29537-3; 978-1-118-29538-0 (ebk)

Printed in the United States of America

10 9 8 7 6 5

Book production by John Wiley & Sons, Inc., Composition Services

Updates to this book are available on the Downloads tab at this site: www.wiley.com/WileyCDA/WileyTitle/productCd-1118100786.html. If a Downloads tab does not appear at this link, there are no updates at this time.

To my wonderful sister Natasha, you have been my biggest fan since the day I was born. I am also your biggest fan and admire you immensely! I am in awe as I watch you in your roles as a mom, wife, and daughter. You are my best friend in the entire world. I can't imagine going a day without talking to you, and I hope I never will.

acknowledgments

My family and friends—I'm so lucky to have such a close-knit family and a genuinely close group of friends. Having the most loving circle around me makes me feel like I can accomplish anything!

Steven Grevemberg—For your support, love, and answering "yes" every time I asked, "Would you please take a look at this for me and tell me what you think?" Your honesty has never gone unnoticed and is always appreciated!

Robert A. Flutie, Hillary Polk-Williams, and the team at Flutie Entertainment—I'm not sure what I would do without you. I thank you so much for your support, recommendations, and advice, and for handling every detail of my career. I don't know how you manage to do it all!

Jane Dystel and Miriam Goderich—Thank you for believing in this project and assisting me in making my dream come true.

Lisa Shotland—Thank you so much for all of your guidance and encouragement.

Ken Sunshine, Janell Vantrease, Cassandra Mills, and the rest of the team at Sunshine Sachs—Thank you for doing such a magnificent job spreading the word.

Cindy Kitchel, Pamela Mourouris, Colleen Schumacher, Donna Wright, and John Wiley & Sons—Thank you for the wonderful support and enthusiasm you've given me throughout this entire process.

Deborah Wheatley—For being the best critic a girl could ask for. Thank you for caring enough to tell me the truth.

Aram Youssefian—Your eye for design isn't the only reason we've been working together for the past 15 years. Thanks for dedicating so much of your time to this endeavor.

contents

about the author

I'm a first-generation American; my parents are Cuban, which means that passion and a love of color are in my genes. Where my passions are concerned, interior design is right at the top of my list. I used to help my mother with her decorating and party-planning business, and really saw all that can be done on a tight budget when you focus on small elements that make a big impact. I've made great use of that early experience in every space I've designed.

I broke into TV as a host for series on TLC and MTV. Television is a fun, exciting business, but the best part of my job has always been connecting with the audience and the guests on my shows. The whole time I was working on those programs, I was also working on private design projects—I never dreamed I'd get to do both together. It's incredibly rewarding to interact with people and give them usable, real-world advice on how to improve their living spaces.

To expand my design knowledge, I studied design and became a LEED-accredited interior designer, something incredibly important to me because environmental issues and "green" design are so important for our future. (LEED stands for Leadership in Energy and Environmental Design, an internationally recognized green building certification system developed by the U.S. Green Building Council.)

My background prepared me for the incredibly varied design challenges I tackle on HGTV and in working with my private clients. Along with hosting and designing rooms for *Get It Sold* and *The High-Low Project*, I've had the opportunity to work on HGTV programs like *White House Christmas*, *HGTV's Green Home*, *Bang for Your Buck*, *House Hunters*, *Showdown*, *HGTV'd*, and *Real Estate Intervention*. Fantastic experiences all, and they led to coverage in magazines including *Time*, *USA Today*, *People En Espanol*, *Instyle*, *Esquire*, *People*, *Better Homes & Gardens*, *Elle Decor*, and *Latina*, as well as appearances on *The Today Show*, *The Rachael Ray Show*, *Extreme Makeover: Home Edition*, and *The Nate Berkus Show*. I am also Target's style expert for home. I have had a blast working with the company to come up with easy ways for their guests to design their own spaces.

When I'm not filming or working with a client, I like to relax at home. There are a million and one things to do in Manhattan, but my favorite is unwinding with family and friends as I indulge my other passions—entertaining and cooking.

introduction

You are creative. Even if you don't think so, you are. The reality is, we all have an imagination. It's where our best ideas are born. Being creative is just a matter of finding the right inspiration and an easy method to help you organize and develop your ideas. That's why I wrote this book—I wanted to give you the tools you need to create your ideal home design.

It always surprises me that most people don't think of themselves as creative. There's this mistaken belief that only certain types of people, like designers or writers, are creative. That's just not true. Nobody has cornered the market on great ideas. In fact, one of my favorite parts of working with homeowners is helping them tap into their imaginations and express themselves through their interior designs. I love to give people the tools and encouragement they need to develop their own ideas.

The best tool I give homeowners is what I call "layering." Back when I first started working with clients, I realized that I had to come up with some sort of process that would be successful time and time again. It had to work in any home and for every design challenge, or I'd just be reinventing the wheel for every new project I tackled.

Any interior design is made of decorative elements layered one on top of the other. Every feature—fixtures, surface treatments, furniture, and so on—relates to and affects all the others. Each element rests on top of, or supports, another decorative feature. That's how I created a process that breaks down interior design into individual, step-by-step layers. The way these layers go together provides you with an easy-to-follow road map for developing your own room design. The process is laid out, which leaves you free to focus on using your imagination.

This book is organized according to the sequential layers. I developed it to be followed chapter by chapter, in order. I think that once you build a design in layers, you'll see that it follows a basic logic.

Find the right balance of color, pattern, texture, and form in your space, and the result will be the kind of eye-popping magic that this living room design captures.

I think of it like dressing. Each layer of clothing goes on in a specific order (well, unless you're a rebel pop star). The layer underneath helps support and gives form to the layer on top. The jacket complements the blouse, and your jewelry accents the colors and textures you're wearing. Each layer is in harmony with the next. Makes sense, right?

Interior design is just like that. I develop a room design one basic layer at a time. Yes, some rooms look great painted in subdued colors, and others look best with walls covered in wallpaper or paneling. But the point is that *every* successful interior design includes well-thought-out surface treatments. That's why deciding how to treat the surfaces in your space is one of the steps in layering.

You don't necessarily need bold colors to rock a room design. This sophisticated kitchen lets the view do the talking. Sleek blond cabinetry, granite countertops, and hip lighting fixtures don't hurt the scene, either.

Here's the formula for a bathroom with a real spa feel: neutral colors, natural materials, soft lighting, and uncluttered decor.

The process of designing a space starts with a cold, hard look at the space to identify its pluses and minuses. I always think about who lives there, how they want to use the space, and what are their tastes and preferences. Then I work up a list of design goals. It's pretty hard to decide on individual interior design elements if you don't even know what you want the end result to be. Once I've got a good plan of action and an idea of how the finished space should look and feel, it's just a matter of building the design, layer by layer. My process leads you step by step through the key decisions homeowners have to make (whether they know it or not) in order to create a successful interior design.

Any given stage of the process may be more or less involved. Let's say you're totally happy with all of your furniture. That means that the fifth layer—editing your furniture—is probably going to be quick and simple. On the other hand, if you're ready to update your furnishings, that stage will be a roll-up-your-sleeves experience that will involve making a whole bunch of big decisions. When it all comes down to it, though, it doesn't matter what your particular situation, budget, and tastes are; layering is flexible enough to accommodate all those variables.

Everyone's creative. It's just waiting to come out.

Flexibility is key because every room is unique. It's not just the natural light exposure, shape, and

Luxury in the bedroom is all about soft surfaces and warm textures. Like the headboard, bed linens, upholstery, and rug in this room, a bedroom's surfaces should be soft to the touch while enchanting the eyes.

physical dimensions of the room. How you use your home and how you want it to look and feel is particular to you. I developed the layering method specifically to work anywhere. (Redesign dozens of rooms every year like I do, and you quickly learn the value of flexibility.) Your house, my house, her house—it doesn't matter. My process works for every interior space and any homeowner's taste. I've used this technique in so many rooms and houses that I've lost count. It has never failed me.

Let's keep in mind, though, that this book is not just about process. Yes, layering is a fantastic way to give your creativity some structure. That's useful, but I also wrote this book to provide guidance and inspiration. You have about a bazillion options when decorating a home. That

translates to a mountain of decisions. I want to help you make confident design choices every step of the way and keep the whole thing fun. That's why, throughout the book, I'll share tips and insights about what has worked for me and what hasn't. I'll give you visual guides to different styles of fixtures, furniture, accents, fittings, and other design elements. You'll even find simple rules that I've learned through trial and error so that you never repeat mistakes I've already made.

So go ahead, turn the page, and jump into layering your own interior space. I know you have all the ideas you need to transform any room in your home and design a look that you'll love. There's no time like the present, and no method like layering, to discover just how creative you can be.

the first layer

understand your space and plan your design

I t's a funny thing: If you live in a house for a while, you simply stop *seeing* it. The interior design turns into a background set to your daily life. That tangle of cables next to the media center becomes invisible. You stop noticing that the chairs on one side of the kitchen table hit the wall whenever they're pulled out, and that your bedroom curtains are so flimsy they don't block out the morning sun streaming through those east-facing windows.

This is the big advantage I have when I walk into a client's house. I clearly see obvious trouble spots—and high points—in a way that the homeowner often can't. It's all fresh to me. I call it the "home-buyer perspective." No matter what room, home, or decorating challenge I'm tackling, I always start with a thorough and brutally honest evaluation of the space.

a fresh start

After hundreds of design projects and years of experience, I have a designer's X-ray vision. I can visually edit out the existing furniture, window treatments, and other features to see the bare bones of a room. Chances are that you've lived in the space you're about to redesign for some time. So I'd like you to clear out the room before you critically assess it.

Yes, that means moving all the furniture out of the space. It's simply the best way to see the space clearly. If you're anything like me, you'll also see it as a great chance to give the room a deep cleaning. It's up to you whether you totally strip the room, taking down wall art and window treatments as well. Take it from me; it's well worth the effort.

Once the room is bare, it's time to channel your inner Sabrina. Grab a notebook or sketchpad, your favorite pen or pencil, and a measuring tape.

(A glass of wine won't hurt the creative process, either.) No matter what, I like to keep it fun. The more enjoyable the process, the more relaxed and creative you'll be. Put on your favorite music, and let's get to it!

Start with the "constants"—the things about the space that you can't change. The first is the floor plan—the positions of permanent architectural and structural elements such as walls, windows, doors, wired-in fixtures, and outlets. Note that the floor plan is different from the layout; the layout is the position of all the design elements in relation to these structural pieces. The floor plan is the foundation on which any interior design is built, and it's going to affect everything in your design to one degree or another.

To get the most out your design, you have to understand the natural light in the space. Chart the natural light throughout the day. Your actual exposure may be affected by external features such as trees or awnings. In any case, daylight has an incredibly powerful effect on how an interior design is perceived, and it's easily one of the most overlooked and misunderstood interior design elements. Where and when sunlight shines into a room is going to determine the best places for TV and computer screens, your choice of color for the space, and a whole lot more. Mark down where the natural light falls. It doesn't take a lot of effort; just walk through the room every hour or so on a normal (not cloudy) day, and mark your sketch with the areas

Previous page: The goal, to create an amazingly stylish kitchen that is easy to navigate, with a clean look and a focus on food prep and cooking. Score!

of morning and afternoon light. It's also a good idea to make notes about areas that stay in shadow all day (those are not the places to park your favorite potted plants!). This knowledge will come in mighty handy, especially when you're picking wall colors.

Now I'd like you to consider the architectural style. Most home styles are pretty accommodating of whatever interior design you choose. A brick bungalow or split-level ranch doesn't really set a specific tone for the interior design to follow. However, if you happen to own a turn-of-the-century Victorian or some other period style, the architecture is just about guaranteed to influence the interior design. If your home's architecture is distinctive, you have two ways to go: Decorate in the style of the architecture (safer), or purposely contrast that style (riskier—especially if you plan on selling anytime soon). So take a moment and jot down your impressions, if any, of the architecture.

A corner location such as this can be the perfect wide-open kitchen floor plan, leaving plenty of room for multiple people to work in the space at the same time. It's also adaptable; many different shapes of islands could be integrated into this kitchen to supply additional work surfaces and storage.

Hardwood floors are an elegant, durable option, especially for a high-traffic common area such as a living room. The finish can be changed to match a new room design, but the grain remains a scintillating visual.

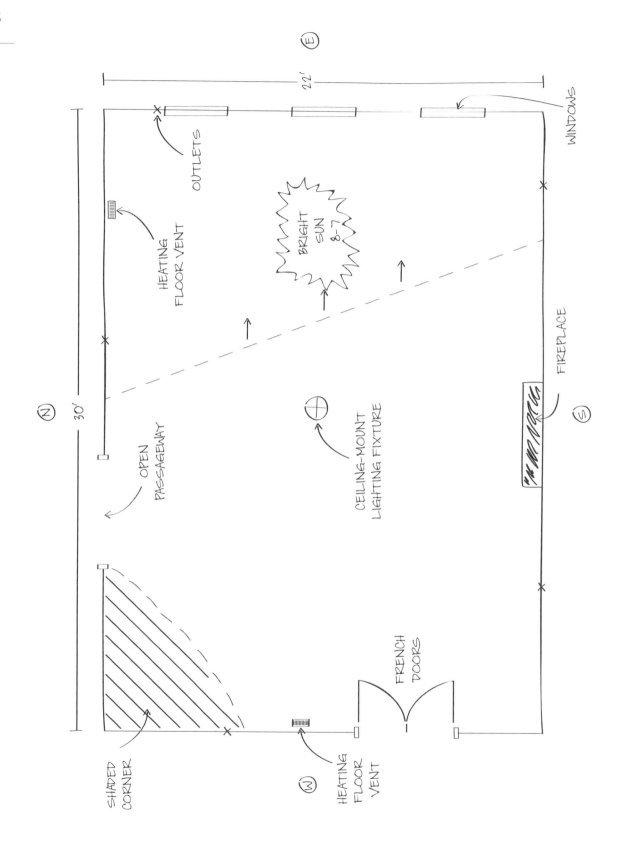

sabrina's rule

SKETCH THE FLOOR PLAN!

Don't even think about launching into a new interior design without a usable sketch of the floor plan. This is a super-important part of the process. Here's the good news: You don't have to be Picasso to make a good, workable sketch. I use a piece of large-format sketch paper because it gives me lots of room to work out potential design features and make notes as I review the space. You can get by with a letter-sized sheet if that works better for you. Some people prefer to use grid paper because the individual blocks provide an easy scale, and whenever you need a straight line, all you have to do is follow the grid lines.

Whatever paper you choose, start your sketch by carefully measuring the space, including the locations of doorways, windows, light fixtures, and outlets. It doesn't have to be pretty, but you do have to mark exactly where all those features are located, as well as the placement of substantial built-ins such as a fireplace or floor-to-ceiling bookshelves. Now all you do is scale down those measurements for your sketch. I use a 1-inch-to-1-foot scale, but you can use whatever scale works best for your sketch—as long as you're consistent and precise. Draw the floor plan by hand, or use a straightedge if you're like me and your straight lines seem to turn into squiggles. Just remember that it doesn't have to be a work of art; it just needs to work. Down the road you're going to put this sketch to use in a number of different ways, to play with furniture positioning and to make other crucial design decisions.

Understanding light exposure is a huge part of interior design planning. These furnishings were placed so that the upholstery would not be faded by the strong sunlight coming in through the southeastern-facing windows.

LISTEN TO THE LINES

Architectural lines affect interior design. At first glance, you may not even notice lines. They aren't a big factor in a basic, unadorned, boxy room. But in some rooms, moldings, casement (the trim around doors and windows), columns, and built-in features such as floor-to-ceiling fireplace structures bring a lot of lines to the look. An abundance of vertical lines gives a room a formal feel and makes it seem more spacious. Horizontal lines create a more relaxed and cozy feel. Curving lines (arched window and door openings, curved steps leading from one room to other) create an informal appearance that seems both unstructured and spontaneous. Be aware of any obvious impact the linear elements have on the look and feel of the space. You can then build on that tone, or use other design elements to counteract it.

Strong vertical lines in moldings, brickwork, and flooring reinforce this hallway's formal appearance. An abstract sculpture, plants, and a beautiful hanging light with an enchanting curved shape help soften the look.

your space, through fresh eyes

Now comes a little bit of a challenge. Pretend you're a home buyer. Start to identify the positives and negatives in the space. The trick is to look at the space as if you've never seen it before—as if you're looking to buy and just walked through the front door. I find that it helps if you literally do just that.

Write down particular challenges that jump out at you—the things you'll want your design to solve. Is the room long and narrow? Are the ceilings low? Is the space naturally dark and shadowed? Do the corners look dingy? Are the windows plain and uninteresting? And what about the surfaces in the room? Are you dealing with aging wood paneling or timeworn carpet? Are there cracks in the wall from the house settling? Are doorways out of square for the same reason?

Don't just stop at what you see; use all your senses (well, don't taste anything). Does the space seem noisy, with lots of surfaces that amplify sound? Does it seem cold because of an abundance of smooth, reflective surfaces? Do the floorboards creak? There are many design solutions for all of these problems, but you have to be aware of a problem before you can solve it.

Note the positive features as well. Does the room have beautiful crown molding? Do the ceilings soar? Is a hardwood floor hidden underneath carpeting? Do you find the shape of the room visually appealing? Are you blessed with stunning picture windows that just need a good cleaning to enhance the view? Are there built-in features that you can play up in the design, or even use as focal points? Do you have a long, unbroken wall space to work with? Noticing the advantages that a space presents gives you the chance to exploit them. You're getting all this down in your notes, right?

If you listen, the existing architecture may speak loudly about the potential design style. The formal wall moldings and highly detailed tray ceiling led to the choice of classic roll-arm furnishings and the use of bolsters in this living room.

Linger. Really get a sense of the space as it is. You might be surprised at what you notice.

Once you get a handle on all those factors you can't change, it's time to start noting what you *can* change. For starters, pick a general tone for your design. What mood and feel do you want in your space? It might sound a little touchy-feely, but this part of the design process is really important because it determines how the space will impact your life. The tone you choose for the space will help you make a lot of design decisions.

I recently redesigned a bedroom for a business executive who is incredibly busy. She works a billion hours a week and moves a thousand miles

an hour, and part of the reason I was there was because she has zero time to think about home design. It was obvious that what she needed was a serene oasis where she can get away from the pressures in her life. It was easy to describe the space: calm, calm, and calm. It had to be peaceful and stress-free. (Stop me if any of this sounds familiar.) It had to be a place for her to hide away, recharge her batteries, and always feel comfortable. That led me to use subtle, soft blue hues, with clean white accents and lots of comforting natural textiles. Everything in the space absorbed sound and felt soft to the touch. I added soft lighting provided by lovely, understated bed table lights, and gave her tons of pillows. Cool closet organizers magically decluttered the whole room and made everything from clothes to linens easy to store and intuitive to find. I even introduced some aromatherapy elements. The client "got it" the moment she walked in; she went right to the bed, kicked off her shoes, and lay down. The moral of the story is that mood is both the beginning and the end point on the map of your design. Take a little time to really capture in words the tone you're after.

A fresh perspective and a well-thought-out plan are the seeds of any successful interior design.

It helps if you think about the design style that suits you—who you and your family are and how you live. Are you young, hip, an early adopter of technology? This can translate to adventurous color schemes, modern furniture, and gear-driven family rooms. Are you more conventional, and do you want your home to be restrained and subtle? Or do you want to be stimulated by your home (bold colors, lots of patterns)? Is comfort the key (overstuffed furniture, soft floor coverings, luxury bathroom fixtures)? How much do you entertain (large dining table, lots of storage)? How much do you cook (gourmet kitchen)? What do you like to do when you're home—sit around and read, watch TV, or even work at home (home office designed into a corner of the living room)? Add to your notes a description of your personal style and the way you want to use your newly designed space. You're going to put all those words to good use a little later on.

sabrina's tip

FIND YOUR PERSONAL STYLE

It's easy to get lost on your way to defining style; I've seen it happen many times. The trick is to take a look at your personal preferences and let them lead you to the style that best suits both your home and your life. Use these questions as prompts for refining your aesthetic and living preferences into a concise design style.

- Are you the type who loves winter and really enjoys hunkering down with a cup of coffee and a good book while it snows outside (overstuffed furniture, plush textiles, warm and dark color schemes)? Or do your prefer the heat of summer and lounging around a swimming pool or grilling out (light or cool colors, shiny tiled surfaces)?
- Are you managing a chaotic tribe (easy-to-clean flooring, surfaces, and finishes; durable wood furniture)? Or are you a single person or a working couple (high-end furnishings, delicate window treatments in luxurious fabrics, hallmark design pieces)?
- Is your eye drawn to uncomplicated lines, minimal ornamentation, and open, expansive floor plans (modern style), or are you more attracted to a space filled with memories, including collections, family photos, kids' artwork, and meaningful accents (country, funky, eclectic styles)?
- Are you drawn to the beauty of wood furnishings, trim, cabinetry, and surfaces, with straightforward design and fine craftsmanship (Prairie or Craftsman style)? Or does your taste run to elegant period colors, highly detailed and dainty furnishings, ornate trim and casework, and plaster wall and ceiling accents (historical period styles)?

For now, round out your initial notes with your impressions of the fixtures in the space and the furnishings you'd like to see. Does the overhead light look like it's straight out of a bad 1970s movie? (It's okay; we've all been there.) Are there drag marks in the floor left over from moving day? Have the cabinets simply become impossible to clean and make look like new? Do you feel like a new coffee table would bring your sofa back to life? Make a list of everything that you think will need to be replaced, covered up, or repaired.

See how well you're getting to "know" your space? It probably already looks different to you.

create a design journal

All those notes you've compiled—along with your floor-plan sketch—form the core of what I call a Design Journal. Putting this plan together should be fun because it's going to be your home-design dream guide and decorating road map all in one. Not only do you need all the background information you've just put together—the positives and negatives of the space and its physical dimensions—but you'll also use the journal to collect ideas that catch your fancy in one easy-to-access place. Your journal will hold and organize clippings from magazines (and maybe even pages from books), paint and fabric swatches, and other inspiration sources

An exposed-beam, wood paneled ceiling combine with high-end raised-panel cabinetry, granite surfaces, and restaurant-quality stainless steel appliances to give this kitchen a theme that can be best described as "opulent country," both upscale and invitingly warm.

such as postcards or even flower petals. You need a way to organize possible sources for different decorating elements. When I make up a Design Journal, I even include photos I've taken of the space and pictures of fixtures and other elements that grab my eye.

I keep a Design Journal for all my projects. I used to use ginormous binders to organize all the information. Nowadays, though, I'm an electronic gal. I scan reference photos, swatches, magazine pages, and other sources of inspiration. I download photos from my digital camera, including shots I've taken in stores of displays, accents, fixtures, furniture, or anything else that seems like it might work in the space I'm designing. I even take photos at friends' houses when I see something I like. I keep all the visuals in a computer file folder along

with a document containing all my notes. It's a great way to organize information, thoughts, and ideas about a decorating project.

You might prefer a low-tech approach, and that's totally fine. If you're more comfortable with a physical journal, use an accordion file or a thick notebook with lots of pockets. Pick something that's fairly easy to take with you when shopping. No matter what you use, the point is to have one single place where you *organize* all your thoughts and inspirations. Take it from me, one of the worst feelings in the world when you're trying to create a dynamite room design is knowing that you've come across the perfect window treatments or light fixture in a magazine, but having no idea where you might have put the picture.

This homeowner was clearly after a modern look, which was achieved with the choice of a highly stylized lighting fixture, streamlined furnishings, and a lack of ornamentation. The more you can define your own style, the easier it will be to implement in a room or house.

A clear and direct design philosophy is easy to decode. The aim here was quite plainly to create a peaceful bathroom decor centered on the simple luxury of a soaking tub. Natural colors, uncomplicated lines, and an uncluttered design all support that aim.

It's always better to make a design decision before your wallet chooses for you.

There's one last thing you absolutely have to add to your journal: a budget. Though nobody likes budgeting, I can't tell you how many times I've watched a home design project go off the rails because the homeowner ran out of money halfway through decorating the space. It's one of those things that kills your creativity, and it can be extremely defeating. So determine the absolute maximum amount you can spend. As you firm up your plans, you'll use your journal to keep track of costs. That way, you can adjust your budget on the fly as you develop your design. A little bit of budgeting will make it obvious that you can't have that sleeper sofa you covet *and* the blown-glass pendants *and* the new carpeting. Something will have to give, and it's always better to make a design decision before your wallet chooses for you.

mission: possible!

I'm betting that by now you've got a great feel for what you like and don't like about the space you're planning to decorate, and what will and won't be possible. You've made a ton of observations, and you should have a lot of great notes. Now we're going to distill all that into a set of design objectives. We'll use those objectives to wrap up your goals into one nice package in a *mission statement* that will guide your project.

I understand that this might sound like a little much, but you'll have to trust me. The more you can refine and clearly state exactly what it is you want your space to do and look like, the more likely you are to end up with a space that looks exactly like what you imagined.

Glance over the notes you've already made, and start writing an "I want" list. These goals should be both functional (how and what you want to do in the space and how you want other people to interact with it) and aesthetic (how you want the space to look and feel). To help you, here are a few of the goals I jotted down during a conversation with a couple whose combination living room and family room I redesigned recently. The goals are actually paraphrases of quotes from the couple:

> "I want . . . the clutter to go away."
>
> "I want . . . a comfortable, good-looking room to relax in with my friends after the kids go to bed."
>
> "I want . . . a separate, designated area for toys that can be disguised on special occasions like holidays."
>
> "I want . . . blues, lots of blues."
>
> "I want . . . a bright and airy look, even when the weather isn't."

I consider the "I want" goals to be yardsticks by which you measure every choice you make.

You get the picture. You just need to identify the key points you're after. As simple as these goals might be, they are crucial in helping you make the right decisions for your design. For instance, given the previous list, it was clear to me that I didn't need to bother with deep, dramatic paint colors or formal, dark-wood furnishings. The couple's simple goals led me to the design decisions I made. I consider the "I want" goals to be yardsticks by which you measure every choice you make. Plus, it's fun and empowering to say out loud what you want in your design.

With your goals and desires for the new design clearly stated, you've set a great foundation for making decisions that will lead to the look you want. Now it's time to start making those decisions, beginning with the all-important issue of the colors that will fill your space.

the second layer

choose your colors

Next to light, color is the most intense and powerful interior design element. Nothing has a bigger impact on how your home looks and how successful any interior design is. I love color because I know from experience the wonderful ways it can transform a home's interior. Most designers are the same way. Unfortunately, a lot of people aren't. More often than not, people are a little scared of being adventurous with color. But you shouldn't be. There are simple and reliable ways to find the colors that are just right for you and your space.

The power of color involves a lot more than meets the eye. Colors have the potential to make an interior seem small or large, cool or warm, cozy or airy. They are also ripe with meaning. Certain colors—everyone has their favorites—bring up emotions and memories. The right color can make you happy for no apparent reason. A different one can make you want to leave a room. Color can even have a physical effect. A room painted deep red has been shown to actually speed up the heart rate, while mid-range green has the opposite effect. In fact, architects and designers tap that influence all the time. Architects regularly use whites and neutrals in airports to help counteract the stress and chaos of air travel. (Now if they could only find a color that would get you through security without all the hassle!)

Colors also have cultural significance that we tend to take for granted because they are so much a part of who we are. No one blinks twice when an American bride wears white for her trip to the altar. But it would be shocking in India, where most brides wear red. We wear black to mourn, while Chinese Buddhists go through the same grieving process wearing yellow. The great kaleidoscope looks very different depending on what part of the world you call home.

Specific colors relate to different periods in history. There is a palette for Colonial America, and you'll find distinctive combinations that define other historical eras right up to the present day. The 1960s were about primary colors and paisley patterns. And who could forget (much as we'd like to) the avocado green kitchens that are so evocative of the '70s?

The truth is, color is part decorative element, sometimes a visual trick, and always a psychological trigger. But above all else, color in interior design is fun. Working with color is my favorite part of designing, and one of my favorite parts of life. Developing your ideal interior color scheme should be fun!

Heck, the hard work has already been done for you. Designers, artists, and other experts long ago figured out the various effects of color on a space. That leaves you to focus on choosing the hues that serve you best and make you happiest. Let's break down the general guidelines so you can choose your own dynamic palette with confidence.

Previous page: A restful mid-range green is the perfect color for a bedroom. Running the color into the bathroom ensures that the spaces are visually unified.

Colors don't have to be brightly jewel-toned to carry incredible power. As the mix of cream, dark browns, and golden browns in this room demonstrate, darker and neutral colors have serious visual weight that makes an unforgettable first impression.

color rules, color realities

There are "rules" about color, and there are realities. I'm betting you've come across some of the rules already: Always paint a room white if you want to make it look larger; lighter is always better; never use colors that clash; and on and on. Fact is, there's no hard-and-fast way to work with color. Name a rule, and somebody has broken it to spectacular effect. The basic underlying principles—the "realities"—that guide the use of color are something else altogether. Ignore the realities and you may wind up spinning your wheels in trial-and-error land.

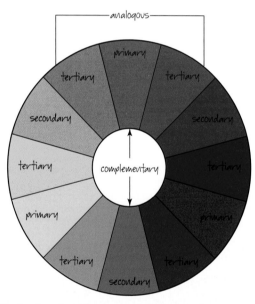

The basic color schemes are all about color interactions around the color wheel.

You can't mess with color realities (like, say, that light colors show more dirt than dark colors). So we might as well start with the basics that everybody agrees on.

There are three *primary* colors: red, blue, and yellow. This basic trio is usually represented by pie shapes spaced equally around a circle, on what we all know and love as the basic color wheel. Mix each of these colors with one another

and you get orange, violet, and green, the *secondary* colors. Six *tertiary* colors are formed by pairing each color with its adjacent colors. You can keep going, mixing colors to finer and finer degrees of separation, but these twelve form the common color wheel. The color wheel helps the uninitiated make successful combinations. Most professionals and avid decorating enthusiasts carry the relationships around in their heads, but make no mistake, they are constantly using the basic principles.

Color rules are pretty fundamental. So let's jump right into the effects different colors have on the perception of a home's interior. Dark colors close off a space reducing the amount of light reflected in the room, making it appear smaller. Light colors, however, open a space up. In other words, if you want a room to look larger, paint the walls a lighter color, and use lighter-colored furnishings and accents. If the ceiling is too low, you should do what? That's right: Paint it a lighter color.

Use this effect to serve your design needs. Make a long, narrow room seem wider by painting one or both end walls a darker color than the side walls (Note: It doesn't even have to be a "dark" color— just a darker color than the one used on the side walls). The end walls appear closer, making the room seem like more of a square than a rectangle. You can make any large room seem cozier by doing the opposite.

Darker colors also absorb more light, which means that if you're using a dark color scheme in a room, you'll likely need more—or stronger— lighting fixtures. On the other hand, any color covered in a high-gloss sheen (gloss paint, silk duvet, or polyester carpet, for example) will look both lighter and less saturated than that same color in a matte surface.

Colors also influence the perception of temperature in a room. Red, orange, and yellow are warm colors. Blues, greens, and violets are cool colors. Warm hues evoke fire, the sun, and, well, heat. Cool colors are just the opposite (think water or a lush lawn).

The "temperature" affects how a space actually feels. That's why in hotter climates, homes often feature color schemes dominated by cool blues, greens, or whites to counteract to some degree the effects of consistently hot temperatures. In a snowy part of the country, a warm color scheme can liven up a home and make it seem more welcoming during the chilly months. Warm colors are called *advancing colors* because, just like dark hues, warm colors make a surface appear closer. Cool colors are called *receding colors* following the same logic. In general, warm colors are considered cozier and welcoming, while cool colors are considered more subtle and sophisticated.

the special case of non-color colors

White, black, and gray are achromatic. That means that they are not one color or another. Black is the result of all colors combined, and white is the absence of color. Gray is a blend of black and white. Solid color theory, but remember color reality? Well, here's a reality check. Today's sophisticated paint-mixing and dye-blending technologies mean that many blacks, whites, and grays are created with undertones of a given color. This isn't a big deal until you try to use black, white, or gray in a space with other colors. You may find these hues that are supposed to work with all colors don't work with yours. Always study the blacks, whites, and grays you're considering and determine whether they have undertones of blue, green, or red. When they don't, they are considered truly neutral.

Which brings us to my friends—the neutral colors. These are technically colors created by combining two complementary colors. The combination "neutralizes" the polarizing power of either color. However, most designers consider black, white, gray, taupe, browns, and off-whites (creams) to be neutral. They work with most other colors.

A wonderful yellow checkerboard floor is the perfect complement to the broad use of white throughout this kitchen. The white keeps the space looking clean and bright, and the yellow adds happy splashes of color.

Wood surfaces are natural complements to a neutral color scheme. Let grain pattern and color variation play off surfaces in shades of brown and taupe, and bingo, a warm, comfortable kitchen perfect for informal get-togethers.

The powder blue, white, and chocolate brown color scheme is a big part of this 1940s-style glamour decor. The colors are perfectly balanced and exactly the right hues for reinforcing the pure fun of the look.

when colors meet

Unless you're a white-on-white-on-white person, sooner or later you're going have to manage the interaction of two colors. Certain colors create interesting visual effects when combined. Many color interactions are fairly self-evident when they happen, and a lot of people encounter them simply by accident. Interactions will influence which color works best as the most prominent, and where you place a given color.

The law of mutual opposites (my special name for it) dictates that when you place a small area of a light color against a bigger area of a dark color, the smaller area will appear lighter than it really is. A small area of dark color against a larger area of light color will seem darker than it really is. To put it in practical terms, if you're picking out orange silk throw pillows for a deep blue couch, they are going to look perceptibly lighter when you get them home and toss them on the sofa than they did in the store.

Color is the 900-pound gorilla of interior design and the perfect way to make a design all your own.

sabrina's rule

KNOW YOUR COLOR VOCABULARY

Being fluent in the language of color can be a big help when you're trying to find just the right slipcover or wall paint. A few key terms are all you need to navigate your way around a paint, fabric, or furniture store.

Hue: The technical name of a color. Primary red is "red." Persimmon would be called "red-orange." This is important because the names retailers give colors are arbitrary and differ from one supplier to another.

Pure or basic: The term for a color in its fundamental form—untinted, unshaded, and unaltered. A pure color is one of the twelve colors comprising the common color wheel.

Shade: Add black to a color and boom, you get a *shade*. A shade is a darker hue of any given color. You can shade to almost infinite degrees of variation.

Tint: Add white instead of black, and you get a *tint* of that color.

Value: The relative lightness or darkness of a color.

Set splashes of bright color against a large white background to not only make the colors really pop, but as a way to moderate the more powerful hues and keep them from overwhelming the room.

A neutral or gray tone placed near a strong color will take on the undertones of that color's complement (the color directly across from it on the color wheel). So if you hang black-and-white photos with wide gray matting on a large wall of green, the matting may appear to have reddish undertones. In most cases, the effect won't be overwhelming, but if the color of a decorative element looks a bit off, check out the surrounding colors. They may be having an effect on the perception of that color.

One last tidbit about color combinations: A color used next to its complement will tend to look brighter and pop more than the same color used next to an analogous (a color right next to it on the color wheel) or neutral color. For instance, a blue couch placed against an orange wall will look brighter and more intense than it would when placed against a green wall. The point is that you can't pick colors solely on theory. You always have to weigh them against each other.

Colors are dynamic. They can surprise you when you put them together or when you light them differently. With that in mind, it's time to look at the most commonly used interior color schemes before we launch into choosing the best colors for you and your interior.

a cornucopia of color schemes

Have you ever noticed how jazz musicians can take a basic song and make it their own? Ultimately, you can do the same with a color scheme, riffing on the underlying logic just like a jazz musician takes liberties with a musical score. Of course, just as a musician doesn't stretch the underlying logic until he understands it, you need to know how basic color schemes work. The ones I've listed here are the most common.

This modern living room clearly illustrates a couple of color interactions. The panel over the round fireplace is placed against a large yellow-cream wall, making the gray look darker and bluer (the yellow's complement) than it otherwise would. The pictures pop out from the light gray, looking darker than they would against a dark gray, and consequently carrying more visual weight and power.

- **Complementary schemes** combine colors that sit right across from each other on the color wheel. Think red and green (hello, Christmas!), and blue and orange. When matched correctly, these combinations set up exciting, eye-pleasing contrasts. The combination creates interesting visual tension. Designers use lots of variations on complementary color schemes, including *split complementary* schemes based on a color and the two colors that sit on either side of its complement, such as blue-violet, yellow, and orange. Regardless, these schemes are usually the most challenging; there is a lot of potential for them to look too busy. That doesn't mean you shouldn't use a complementary scheme, just be careful when choosing the colors. I like complementary colors in active social areas. Living rooms, dining rooms, and even large kitchens are faves for this scheme.

- **Analogous schemes** are the go-to option for many people. They combine colors (usually three) that sit right next to one another on the color wheel. An analogous scheme is easy to manage and sets up less dynamic tension than a complementary scheme. That doesn't mean they aren't interesting. Consider the warm analogous scheme that includes yellow, chartreuse (yellow-green), and amber (yellow-orange). That'll get your engine going. These schemes translate well to just about every room and are easy to work with. They're also a great option if you want an all-warm or all-cool color palette.

- **Triad schemes** can be stunning when done right . . . but are color chaos when they miss the mark. These schemes use three colors spaced equidistant around the color wheel. It's important that the colors be exactly equidistant from each other, because a little off one way or another and you'll be asking for a color mulligan. The combination of primary red, blue, and yellow is probably the best-known triad. *Tetrad* schemes are triads taken one step further—four colors spaced equally around the color wheel. Triads work best in larger, multipurpose rooms, like combination living

A teal piece of art appears muted placed against the analogous chartreuse wall. The lighter green also makes the blue appear darker. Yes, it's a bit bold, but it's a very sophisticated color scheme in which the profusion of bright white acts like a referee between the two other colors, moderating their impact.

room-family rooms. It's best to have plenty of room to blend hues and play with the color relationships across furnishings, textiles, and surfaces. Green, purple, and orange are an example of a triadic scheme.

- **Monochromatic color schemes** feed a passion for a single color and are perhaps the easiest to put together. Not to be confused with *monotonal*—which uses one basic color at the same strength throughout a room—monochromatic schemes use a single color and shades and/or tints of that color. The knock on these color combinations is that they can be boring; but one person's boring is another's Zen. Create visual excitement by using greater tonal variations between the color and shades and tints. Ramp up the look even more by introducing patterns and lines.

- **Achromatic schemes** consist of white, black, and gray and are remarkably easy and fool-proof. Most people find the lack of true color a drawback, and achromatic schemes have a tendency to appear austere and sterile. However, this can be a stunning palette for a modern space, especially when accented with tiny splashes of bold color in vases, candle-sticks, or other accents. Achromatic schemes also work great in transitional spaces between much more colorful rooms.

- **Neutral schemes** are usually either analogous, monochromatic, or a combination. They are safe combinations that are forgiving of differ-ences in lighting and other variations such as surface sheen. Neutrals work exceptionally well for transitional spaces, such as small entryways and hallways. However, like a monochromatic scheme, a combination of purely neutral tones can be somewhat unexciting. That's why I like to go to one end or the other of the neutral spectrum—think deep, rich chocolate brown or golden sand. The right neutral scheme cre-ates a welcoming sense of comfort in a living room, dining room, entryway, or hall.

Obviously, there are several ways to put colors together so that they play nice and provide a pleasing, long-term look. When you pick your colors, you'll use one of these standards, or a variation. Stick to the underlying principles and you'll wind up with color combinations you love that blend well in your space.

A great way to create an eye-pleasing living room: Combine the basic analogous duo of green and blue against a backdrop of white. It's clean and easy to put together, and makes for a truly pleasing living room.

A single (or monochromatic) color—especially beige, like this living room—is ideal for a formal look. The sophisticated style is reinforced by chic textures, simple lines, and a symmetrical layout. The appearance is cool, calm, and collected.

This living room features a sophisticated twist on the classic blue-and-yellow complementary pairing, incorporating subtle tones of gold and yellow mixed with various blues, all against a neutral backdrop of browns and whites.

Neutral light brown provides the perfect backdrop as the primary color in this scheme. White serves as a secondary color, and dark brown is used as an accent color.

the system of trios

Color theory is all well and fine, but there comes a time when you're ready to choose a color scheme. I've come up with a simple system to help you do just that.

I like to keep things simple, especially when it comes to providing a tool that can be used right away. That's why I use the *System of Trios* (often called the 60-30-10 rule, representing the ideal coverage of each color in a scheme). Here's how it works: First, you select a primary or theme color to cover the largest physical area. Then you choose the color that will have the second-most coverage (the secondary or supporting color). Finally, you pick the color that will be used the most sparingly in the space, the accent color.

Let's be clear here: This is all about using three colors in a specific relationship to each other. The trio forms the core of your interior color scheme.

It's a fantastic starting point, and for a lot of clients I've worked with, it's an ending point as well.

However, I've had clients get overly literal with the system. They start sweating that the floor color isn't one of the colors they've chosen, or that green houseplants might clash with their trio. Remember that this whole process is supposed to be fun. The System of Trios is a way to choose the main colors for your scheme. Usually, wood flooring is neutral enough to fit in with just about any color scheme. If the finish on your floor clashes with the three colors you've chosen, you can use a rug to moderate the effect. Plants blend in seamlessly with most room designs. The point is that you can't and shouldn't control every single color that is introduced into the space. You should only focus on the overall scheme.

The big step in using trios is deciding which color will be the primary. People are usually

At first glance, a dark floor might seem counterintuitive in this bright and cheery kitchen. In reality, the deep brown, wood-grain laminate flooring provides a strong foundation for the room design and makes the white and green colors really pop.

most comfortable using the lightest or least brilliant hue as the primary, with the boldest, brightest, or strongest color reserved for accents. The strongest visual—the most dynamic color—draws the eye (even though you still "read" the entire color scheme). Safe as it is, that's not the only way to go. You can reverse the conventional relationship and make the most visually arresting color your theme color, accenting with the lightest or least dramatic color. See how that works? The accent still draws the eye, but the perspective of the entire scheme is exactly opposite of what the mind expects. This illustrates why the System of Trios is like an Olympic gymnast—super flexible.

A funky mod kitchen is well served by the surprising combination of dark chocolate brown (primary), bright white (secondary), and electric orange (accent). One of the great things about color trios is that a single exciting color can turn around an otherwise sedate pair of hues.

This living room features a complex color scheme with dark green as the predominant color, an analogous orange paired with a lighter tint of that green, and beige and white moderating the colors.

Trios work perfectly when slotted into any of the general color schemes. Most, like a split complementary scheme, naturally involve three colors. The first color chosen is often a natural primary color. Monochromatic schemes lend themselves to a basic color, a tint, and a shade (the shade is normally the primary, the basic color the secondary, and the tint the accent). Analogous schemes are also usually three colors, as are achromatic schemes (white, black, and gray, remember?).

It's a pretty easy system to get your head around, but don't feel limited. The system is an easy way to develop a successful core palette. If you feel comfortable introducing a fourth color, by all means do it! It's your home. They're your colors. You're going to live with them, and I want them to make you happy. Just stick to the logic of whatever scheme you've chosen.

nine tried-and-true trios

Here are nine color combinations from the System of Trios archives. This is just a sampling; there is no limit to the number of three-color combinations you can come up with. I've listed the combinations in order of coverage: primary, secondary, and accent.

1. simply sophisticated

This would be considered a neutral scheme (technically, it's achromatic), but it's not Switzerland neutral—it's got some bite to it. Black accents pop against the white and gray, but the softer two colors create a very elegant backdrop. It's a lovely combination for a low-key formal living room, a modern den, or a well-appointed but minimal guest bedroom. The scheme looks best with solid-color upholstery and either period or modern wood or leather furnishings. Overstuffed floral couches or retro gear will look odd against this trio. I like to introduce transient splashes of color with flowers or candles.

Flannel gray + White + Black

2. fire and ice

Complementary colors seem like a contradiction: opposites that go well together. I like to use black, white, or gray as a bridge between complementary colors. The gray here could easily be replaced with white for a lighter, brighter effect. Complementary schemes work best where they have enough space to spread out and allow you to fine-tune the balance between colors. I would use this particular scheme in a living room or a large guest bedroom.

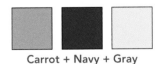

Carrot + Navy + Gray

3. cool haze

This monochromatic scheme resonates with people who love blue (and there are many of them). The colors are well balanced, just different enough to keep the look interesting without venturing too far into a shrill light blue on the one end or an overly deep purple on the other. This combo is perfect for an adult bedroom, a large bathroom, or even a larger transition space. Replace the lavender with bright white for a wonderful kitchen color combo.

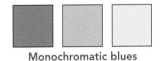

Monochromatic blues

4. girl's got game

A young girl's room is a great place to get a little wild with color. Girls love color extremes. Because the room will change as she grows, you don't have to worry about the colors getting old in the long run. This high-energy trio is a lot of fun to work with. The dialed-back yellow calms the other two colors just enough to make the look work. I bend the trio philosophy here and echo the primary and secondary colors throughout the room's accents (there tend to be a lot of decorative elements in a girl's room). Don't be afraid to introduce patterns such as striped bed linens, curtains, or fun wall art.

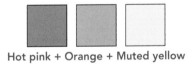

Hot pink + Orange + Muted yellow

5. soothing satisfaction

I like to call this my "spa" color scheme. Sometimes you just need a restful retreat, a calm space where you can recharge your batteries. This easy-on-the-eyes trio provides the perfect palette for relaxing and rejuvenating your spirit. It is also a fairly elegant scheme that stands the test of time and works well with many different furnishing styles. It's wonderful in a bedroom, a formal living room, a large entryway, or a subdued dining room design.

Linen white + Gray + Slate

6. neutral warmth

One of the great things about neutral colors is that you can warm them up or cool them down by adding undertones of a warm or cool color. This means you can adapt a neutral scheme you love to the pre-existing tone of your home—whether you've chosen a cool Mediterranean vibe or a hot Southwestern flair. This particular trio has cool undertones but creates the coziness and comfort associated with warmer schemes. (Colors can be magical!) It's a restful combination, but with enough variation to be visually interesting over time. I've used this palette in smaller bedrooms, living rooms, and dens.

Cream + Brown + Tan

7. stately softness

The teal in this mix always throws people off when I suggest it. Visions of oversized Santa Fe jewelry and swimming pool liners must pop into their imaginations. But this particular teal is muted— it's much nicer than you might think when spread over a large surface such as walls or a rug. The teal is moderated by the ivory, which is just off-white enough to soften the look of the whole room. The navy pops against the other two colors and makes lamps, artwork, and other decorative features come toward you. This is one of my more interesting schemes, and I wouldn't hesitate to use it in a bedroom, dining room, or living room.

Muted teal + Ivory + Navy

8. not your mother's browns

There are browns, and then there are rich, deep browns. The browns in this variation on a neutral scheme are some of my very favorites; they are so sumptuous that they seem almost edible. Dark browns can seem overly somber, but not here. The light gold-brown brings some zip to the look. This trio works great in a nontraditional den, a living room in a home featuring neutral schemes in other rooms, or a dining room.

Earth tones

9. super citrus

You can almost taste the tang of this light, bright color scheme. Midrange yellow and green are analogous, and the bright white keeps the peppier colors from overwhelming the space. It's a happy, perky combination that leans toward the warm side of things. This is a great mix for a modern or contemporary kitchen, or even an older kitchen that you want to update in a fun style.

Lemon + Lime + White

color room by room

The colors throughout a home should tie together in one way or another, but I believe each room deserves its own color treatment. You're going to use different rooms in unique ways, and the lighting varies greatly from space to space. You'll see the colors in a bedroom mostly under artificial light, but you'll use your kitchen day and night, so you'll be exposed to the colors in daylight and under artificial lighting equally. All this variation calls for color solutions specific to each room.

Color rules are broken as often as they are followed.

My suggestions come from my experience in designing and decorating vastly different rooms. It's all about what I've seen work most often. That said, these suggestions aren't the law of the land. Remember what I said at the beginning of this chapter: Color rules are broken as often as they are followed. Just make sure you keep in mind the sound reasoning we've already covered and have a method to your madness. You should be able to explain—at least to yourself—which colors will fill the primary, secondary, and accent roles and why.

● Transitional areas. I'm a firm believer in neutral or near-neutral transitional areas. Hallways, small foyers, and passageways should be less about making a design statement than about setting the stage for the color scheme in the room you're entering. The truth is, most transitional spaces have modest lighting that doesn't show vibrant colors to their best advantage. Deep, dark, or dramatic colors can make these spaces seem claustrophobic. The one exception that I make is entryways that are large enough for people to linger. Even there, though, I often suggest incorporating at least a shade or tint of the primary or

Blond cabinets and flooring provide a neutral base for a sharp, clean, analogous kitchen color trio. Bright white adds a clean look as the primary color, while the smaller pops of bright blue and green are just enough to keep the space lively.

White, yellow-cream, and beige are a perfect transitional trio in this open entry space and staircase. The colors are calming and clean, an ideal bridge to other color schemes in the house.

secondary color used in an adjacent room, which creates a strong link and an interesting visual flow for the eyes to follow.

● Kitchen. White is the color of choice for about 80 percent of kitchens in the United States. I'm not opposed to white. It's a clean bridge for the often multiple tones of kitchen cabinetry, flooring, and countertops. This is especially true if you opt for a standout surface such as a Terrazzo countertop. White is also the color of hygiene. That said, you and I both know that you're more exciting than an all-white kitchen. White makes a great primary or even secondary hue, but other colors can add excitement to this largely functional space. I like to use white in the cooking and prep areas, with a strong or vibrant secondary color for the dining area and bold or bright textiles such as chair upholstery and window treatments as accents. Warm schemes are well suited to the space because they add coziness that fosters social interaction. (I don't know about you, but social interaction is what my kitchen is all about.)

Want to keep an all-white kitchen from becoming boring? Use the kind of detailing apparent in this spectacular kitchen outfitted with specialty cabinets, complex moldings, and an incredible ceiling treatment. A stone-tile floor and stylized wood table island break up the intensity of the unbroken white. Incredible vistas and sun exposure are the icing on the cake.

Off-white, black, and wood tones make for a sleek, modern kitchen style that retains a bit of warmth and personality.

- **Bedroom.** The bedroom has always meant two things to me: rest and relaxation. Restful colors are cool, like blue and green. Keep colors neutral or muted, and add pops of bolder color throughout with accents and flowers.

- **Kid's room.** Two words: Go wild. Your son or daughter will want a new look in a few years or less, so a kid's room is a great place to accommodate the occupant's current tastes, no matter how far out those tastes might be. Let your child have some input into choosing the colors (although you should control the overall scheme to make sure it's not a color riot), and be prepared to experiment. Warm colors tend to work best for girls, while boys usually lean toward the cooler end of the spectrum. In these rooms, a complementary color scheme can really answer the call, and bold or fringe colors can find an enthusiastic audience.

sabrina's rule

MAINTAIN COLOR CONTINUITY

You probably aren't designing the whole interior of your home all at once. More likely, you're working in one room or area. If the color scheme is not coordinated with the colors in the rest of your home, you risk setting up a jarring visual contrast from room to room. Fortunately, there are lots of ways to create color continuity throughout a home. One of the easiest is to use the same color on moldings and trim in every room. You can also include a shade of a color used in adjacent rooms as one of your three colors in the new space. Repetitive accents or fixtures are another terrific continuity technique. Regardless of how you establish it, always keep continuity in mind when picking colors.

Bright-white molding is a simple, clean, and time-tested way to create visual continuity from one room to another. It's also a very sharp look in any room.

- **Living room and family room.** I choose common-area color schemes that capture the overall design goals and style and foster the intended use of the space. Throw a lot of parties? Then the room is a candidate for warm colors. A neutral scheme might be more appropriate for a living room in a formal, sophisticated home design. I often look to my clients' art for indications about which colors will work best in their living room or family room. As a general rule, these spaces are great for trying out slightly more adventurous schemes using color families that speak to you personally.

- **Bathroom.** Not all bathrooms are created equal. I don't hesitate to use a strong color in a powder room because people are going to spend very little time there. But a master bath with a spa tub and a separate dressing area is a whole different room. Start with the practical. If you're going to be applying makeup or regularly checking your look in the mirror, I strongly suggest that you go with light colors. Bright, deep, or dark colors can alter your skin tone as you see it in the mirror and can lead to cosmetic mistakes. Because bathrooms are supposed to be private spaces and be restful to one degree or another, I tend to decorate them with cooler colors moderated with white. That's not to say you can't use a warm palette; just keep in mind that your skin tone is likely going to be affected by reflected hues.

a word about pattern

Pattern is a handmaiden to color. Any pattern in an interior space is made up of colors. Some patterns are a mix of many colors, while others are combinations of two colors in a repetitive design. Regardless, the reality (yes, another color reality) is that the farther away you are from a pattern, the more the colors blend into the dominant hue. The same is true for smaller or busier patterns. The busier the pattern is and the more colors in it, the more it will need to be offset by solid hues and simple shapes.

I love patterns, but one of the downsides is that they can date furnishings. They are also more difficult to successfully integrate into an overall color scheme. I don't mean that you have to give up on that plaid wingback chair; you just need to be careful with it. Solid-color furniture is easier to adapt into a room design, but a single patterned piece will work almost

Dark and light beige tones accented with green create a comfy but luxurious bedchamber perfect for sleep. Notice how the wall art stays in the same neutral family.

Don't be afraid to go bold. Here, a pair of canary yellow chairs take their color from an wall-sized original abstract painting.

as easily. The more patterns you have—in wallpaper, upholstery, window treatments, and floor coverings— the more potential you have for unpleasant visual conflict. When I use patterns, I like to use those in which the dominant color matches either the primary or secondary color I've picked for the space. And I always hedge my bets when I pick a pattern for a room. I use patterns where I can swamp them out if they're not working, or if they start to look a little long in the tooth, such as rugs and window treatments.

There are certain accepted ways of working with patterns. In general, large spaces call for large patterns, while smaller patterns should be used in smaller spaces (they blur into a single shape from far away). Simple stripes make an excellent background pattern against which other, more detailed, figural patterns can be placed quite easily, as long as there are no jarring color contrasts between the two.

No matter how you use patterns, they should reflect your color scheme as closely as possible. Of course, that means you have to determine the colors in your scheme!

picking a personal palette

You only have to spend two minutes in front of the paint chips at your local home center to understand the astounding selection of colors available. It's easy to get overwhelmed. Take a deep breath and bring it back to what's important: your colors. Start with your favorite color, if you have one. It doesn't have to be the exact color you wind up using; this is just a starting point. Are you in love with deep purple or neon lime green? Your favorite color tells you what side of the color wheel you're drawn to and gives you a color family (blue in one case, yellow in the other) to start you off.

Now broaden your thinking to colors and combinations that you find inspiring and interesting (get out your Design Journal; you're going want to jot this down). Look at nature, at flowering plants, at fruit, at a sunset or the waves on a beach. See

This "traditional" home office is well outfitted and stylish, rocking a yellow, black, and green color trio. The check pattern on the chairs is just enough to bring some visual energy to the space without making the relatively furniture-heavy room even more graphically busy.

those things for the color combinations they really are. What draws you in? Is it the simple white and blue of a summer sky stippled with cottony clouds? Is it the 101 variations of green in a dense forest? Or is it a display of peonies in full bloom contrasted against foliage and tree bark? Somewhere in the vast palette of nature, you are likely to find a combination that appeals to you.

Some of the most inspiring color combinations I've seen have been on fashion runways.

Even so, don't stop at the great outdoors on your hunt for the perfect colors. Think about fashion—the way a red dress is accented with a black belt and an orange purse in an ad you saw. Some of the most inspiring color combinations I've seen have been on fashion runways. Keep your eyes peeled for combinations that visually stop you in your tracks, or that elicit a specific emotion or strong response.

Cast your net far and wide. Inspiration and brilliant color composition can be garnered from an old movie poster or product packaging. You don't necessarily have to invent a color scheme for your space. Sometimes you just have to reinvent one. These kinds of inspirational moments are why I carry a digital camera with me almost everywhere I go. Just recently in Manhattan I saw a yellow cab parked in front of a building with a storm-cloud gray facade and purple-black awnings over all the ground-floor windows. Click. That combination is going to find its way into one of the rooms I design.

Certain colors will move you. Start identifying specific colors that are candidates for your space, and collect samples whenever possible. They can be paint chips or fabric swatches, or even the side of a pasta box that seems just the right shade of blue for accenting your living room. Whatever the source, start refining your choices to narrow down the type of scheme you want to use and the three colors that fit into that scheme. Once you've made your preliminary choices, you need to test the colors in the space itself. You'll do that with a concept board.

working with a concept board

It's time to take your Design Journal one step further. A *concept board* represents the colors you want to use in the space, in the actual materials. Arrange the material samples in relative proportion to how widely they will be used in the room (a primary color swatch will be larger than one for an accent color). The best way to make a concept board is to use foam core—a lightweight, white mounting board used for presentations (you can find it at art and office supply stores). The bigger your concept board, the better. The more important thing, however, is that the colors be represented accurately. Paint wall color samples directly onto the concept board. Glue down textile samples, such as furniture coverings, drape swatches, and small sections of rug materials and inspirational photos. Position the concept board in the room you're designing and check it out under the room's natural and artificial lighting. Swap out those colors or materials that aren't working for you until you've found your ideal colors. Don't hesitate to make more than one concept board—they don't take much effort, after all. It may sound like a lot of work, but trust me—it's a lot of fun!

When you've found your perfect colors, you'll know it. They'll strike a chord in you. Keep the samples, note particulars like fabric dye lot numbers and paint chip names, and get ready to move forward on your design adventure. Next up: the surfaces that define your space!

A film buff created his own cozy home theater in a family room with a wall mounted flat-screen TV that can be hidden away behind sliding doors, and a projector that drops out of the ceiling and allows for larger format movie viewing.

The concept board for a room as plush as this would include rug, upholstery, drapery, and wall-panel fabric swatches; paint chips; and shade material samples.

Using the natural tones of rich, dark wood as a jumping-off point, this homeowner created a marvelous, masculine home office at one end of a living room. It features a neutral color scheme with dramatically rich hues—taupe, dark brown sugar, and creamy beige.

the third layer
select your surface treatments

Walls, floors, ceilings, and countertops are the package for your interior design. They can serve as a complementary background for other decorative elements, or you can use surfaces as design high notes themselves. That's actually the first question you'll answer about your walls, floors, ceilings, and countertops: Are they backdrops or focal points?

More often than not, people choose the backdrop option. It's a safe way to work. Hey, there's nothing wrong with leaving a surface unadorned—just as long as that decision is intentional rather than accidental. Surfaces are natural supporting elements in an interior design.

Of course, you can take the opposite approach and make one or more of your surfaces a standout feature. There are a head-spinning number of decorative treatments that can make any interior surface beautiful in its own right. It all comes down to serving your design vision without blowing your budget. New surface options are relatively pricey, so you want to make sure that any one you choose brings real bang for your design buck.

Start with the floor. It's the area of an interior design that most often remains unchanged. What you do with the floor will affect decisions you make about the other surfaces in the space. So let's talk style underfoot.

finessing your floor

Even if you decide not to use your floor as a graphic centerpiece, it still has to complement and support your design vision. At the very least, it should present a clean, fresh foundation. The big decision is whether you'll keep the existing flooring or replace it with an updated version.

That depends on what kind of attention you want the floor to draw. Floors in bold, deep, or vibrant colors, or those with dynamic patterns or scintillating color variations, draw the focus away from other decorative elements. Lighter wood floors, monochromatic tiled surfaces, or neutral resilient flooring tend to blend seamlessly into the background. If your floor is drawing attention because of cracks, separations, or the dingy look of defeat that you can't clean away, it's time to replace it or cover it up. No interior design looks complete with a timeworn, visibly degraded floor.

Consider how the room will be used as well. A hard surface such as ceramic or stone tile is undeniably beautiful and can be ideal where water is a concern, but these materials can also be cold, can be less forgiving of dropped breakables, and can make for a noisy room. Wood, laminate, and linoleum floors are soft and warm and present a wealth of potential appearances, but you'll need to take care not to scratch them. Carpeting can be the height of luxury where your toes are concerned, but

Previous page: A brown Marmoleum floor fits right into the neutral color scheme—and natural materials—that distinguish this room design.

It's hard to top an ebony floor, especially with the engaging patterns of wood showing through. Don't let the pattern fool you, though—this floor is laminate.

Want a standout countertop? Try a formed-glass version like the one shown. These can be made to order and are ideal companions for stone floors and other natural surfaces.

A tan stone floor sets the stage for this neutral kitchen design.

The surfaces that define your interior are your biggest canvases. Don't you dare let them be boring.

a houseful of pets or the traffic through a busy room can put the beat-down on a carpeted floor.

Where the existing floor is in great shape and complements the look you're after, stick with it. Just make sure it looks as close to new as possible. Home centers stock a selection of products for sprucing up floors. You'll find wood rejuvenators to bring a hardwood surface back to life, grout cleaners to make a tile floor sparkle, and specialty cleansers to clean stone surfaces. You can also rent carpet shampooers and everything else you'll need to clean fibers underfoot. No matter what type of floor it is, a thorough cleaning gets the room design off to a good start.

Sometimes, though, no matter how hard you try to revive an existing floor, it still looks old and worn. If that's the case, or if your design calls for an entirely different look, it's time to think about a whole new floor.

new floor 411

Back in the day, bathrooms usually included tile or sheet vinyl flooring. Kitchens were tiled, living rooms always had wood floors or carpeting, and bedrooms were generally carpeted. Thank

sabrina's rule
SHOES OFF!

Shoes track soil, allergens, and a whole lot of other nasty stuff into the house. Small, jagged grains of dirt can scar wood floors and degrade the finish. Carpet traps dirt, so much so that it can deteriorate indoor air quality, making allergies and asthma worse. Tracking any kind of dirt over a tile floor speeds grout discoloration. All in all, shoes are bad news for your floors. That's why I always create a space for shoes just inside the entryway of any house (hidden, of course) I work in, and enforce a "no shoes inside" rule.

The rich grain of this hardwood plank flooring perfectly complements the sumptuous interior in this luxurious living room.

goodness we're past all that. These days, a kitchen might feature any number of flooring options, each one as beautiful as the next. The same is true of every other room in the house. It comes down to choosing a floor that gives you the look you want, works with the way you live, and fits your budget. The following section gives the lowdown on the many new-flooring options.

Where carpeting was once a mainstay in the bedroom, laminate is now a popular flooring of choice. As this room shows, you can have the beauty of wood with a soft, warm feel underfoot.

The maple plank flooring in this bright and sunny bedroom has been stained a neutral mid-range brown that would work well with many different color schemes. Finishing it in natural creamy off-white would have worked as well.

The traditional oak strip floor remains a wildly popular option thanks to a handsome face that suits just about any decor. The inherent durability makes this a lifetime floor.

Reclaimed doesn't mean second best. This jaw-dropping floor was created of select hardwoods salvaged from a barn. Notice the different plank widths that add even more visual interest to an already stunning surface.

It's not just distinctive grain and color that makes antique wood flooring so captivating. This oak bathroom floor features the handsome marks of circle sawing, a technique used to cut planks long before modern mechanized processes took over.

sabrina's tip

SALVAGE AND SAVE TWO WAYS

What if I told you that you could help the environment and have an incredibly beautiful wood floor that is one of a kind? What if I told you that you could have this floor for less than the cost of a new wood floor? Well, it's true. Reclaimed wood floors are salvaged from old, dilapidated buildings. Many are incredible wood species—such as wormy chestnut or American black walnut—that are no longer widely available. Most are fantastically beautiful, with amazing grain patterns and dramatic natural colors. Reclaimed wood floors have often been exposed to elements that make the surface incredibly alluring. For instance, tobacco barn wood is salvaged from century-old tobacco curing barns that housed hot, smoky fires. Time, high temperatures, and smoke combined to saturate the wood with compounds that create sensational colors. Depending on the wood and where it comes from, reclaimed flooring can be a bargain. No matter where you get it, reclaimed wood flooring is extremely green because it saves trees from being cut down and keeps waste material out of landfills.

wonderful wood flooring options

Wood flooring is a traditional choice, as popular today as it has been throughout history. Choose from a vast selection of species, and vary the look of your floor even more with the finish you choose or the width of the boards. A parquet floor—wood squares set in an alternating pattern—can jazz up a period or formal interior. Boards in strip floors range from 2½ to 4 inches wide, while plank floors (up to 12 inches wide) are considered a less formal style.

The floor's finish also sets a tone. A completely matte surface leaves the impression of unfinished wood and is a modern look. Of course, the real attraction is the wood itself.

HOMEGROWN HARVEST: HARDWOODS

A pleasing light tan color and even graining make oak the most popular hardwood flooring, but you don't have to limit yourself.

- Oak is the traditional strip wood flooring, used for its even tan-to-cream coloring and its open, flowing grain. Oak is hard and durable, and it takes stain well, so you can choose a light or dark appearance.

- Ash is a great high-traffic flooring because it's extremely hard (it's used in baseball bats). The grain pattern is similar to oak, but the wood is appreciably more yellow. Ash is generally finished in its natural color because it doesn't take stain well.

- Hickory has a less formal look. The wide-open flowing grain pattern varies from board to board. The colors run from a slightly reddish brown to darker areas and stripes, although some hickory is closer to cream and tan. It's usually finished natural.

- Cherry is a favorite among furniture makers and has a tight, smooth, even grain and a lovely light brown color with rich red undertones. Stand a cherry tree next to an oak, and you'll understand why cherry is one of the more expensive hardwoods (a lot less wood per tree). However, it can be stained or finished in many different shades.

- Walnut is a distinctive and alluring wood that is one of my favorites. If offers a dark brown surface shot through with darker streaks and fascinating grain patterns. Pattern and color vary quite a bit from board to board.

- Maple has long been used in fine cabinetry and furniture making. The flooring is attractive for the same reasons woodworkers reach for it—a consistent, rich, creamy blond color and subtle yet interesting grain. Maple is also very durable.

Oak   Ash   Hickory

Cherry   Walnut   Maple

INFORMAL FOOTING: SOFTWOODS

Softwood flooring is easier to dent and scratch than hardwood flooring, but it's less expensive. Softwood surface patterns and colors are considered a casual look, but one that is easy on the eyes.

- **Pine** leads the way among softwood flooring, and southern yellow pine leads the way among pine floors. The wood has a naturally creamy yellow color with a pronounced, almost crude grain pattern. Pine floors are often stained, and occasionally painted. I prefer the plank form used in informal spaces such as a cottage-style living room or a country kitchen–dining room combo.

- **Douglas fir** flooring may lack excitement, but it makes up for it in adaptability. With a tight, uniform grain and an even honey brown color, the wood is an ideal backdrop for many different decors. It is subtle, is relatively inexpensive, and suits both formal and informal spaces. It's also a hard softwood, so it resists denting and scraping.

Pine   Douglas fir

Let me warn you: Wood flooring can be expensive. The cost may seem less significant, though, when you consider that you'll be spending it on a wood floor that will last for decades.

WOOD FLOOR ALTERNATIVES

Engineered wood flooring is a newer, less expensive alternative to real wood, created by layering *plies* of wood or wood byproducts to construct a base for a strip or plank. The board is then topped with thin layers of a specific wood species. Although engineered wood floors resist moisture and other environmental factors better than regular wood flooring, you can only sand and refinish the surface one or two times over the floor's life since it's composed of thin layers.

Bamboo is a fast-growing, super-strong grass, and an environmentally friendly alternative to wood flooring. It is cut and flattened, or strips are laminated together, to create flooring with extremely interesting surface patterns. Bamboo can be stained in the same shades as wood, and it can even be colored. It comes in tongue-and-groove strips that are nailed into place as an oak floor would be; glue-down strips; or strips, planks, and tiles that simply click together over an existing surface. I'd use it in just about any room of the house. Bamboo flooring is, however, softer than wood. Consider using rugs or mats to protect the floor in high-traffic areas such as entryways.

A blond strip floor—especially one with the tight grain shown here—is a sleek, sophisticated look perfect for a clean modern design.

CERAMIC AND PORCELAIN

The great thing about kiln-fired tiles can be summed up in one word: versatility. A floor of pure white 4-inch-×-4-inch tiles is going to give you a clean and plain look fairly inexpensively, but it's easy to spruce up that look. Add a border of hand-painted or specially designed tiles. Use colored tiles to create a kitchen floor in your favorite hue, or use more than one color to create a nearly limitless number of possible flooring patterns.

Tile direction can vary the look as well, creating herringbone, "running bond," and other patterns.

Use larger tiles to make a small room lo[ ] or use mosaic tiles to make the space se[ ] cozier. Pick from the most common shin[ ] finish, unglazed tiles (which may need to[ ] sealed), or a matte finish.

Whichever you choose, tile is durable and easy to work with. Once properly grouted into place, ceramic or porcelain tile floors are virtually waterproof, which accounts for their immense popularity in kitchens and baths. However, the look doesn't translate well to other rooms.

Ceramic tiles can look just like stone at a fraction of the price.

As subtle and understated as the stone's colors are, limestone tiles in varied sizes create a dynamic loft floor that makes a strong case for barefoot living.

STONE

A genuine stone floor screams luxury and permanence. The more extraordinary the coloring, grain, or veining, the more expensive the tiles. You can't top the look, though. Stone comes in all kinds of scintillating colors, from muted creams to understated grays to stunningly vibrant reds and purples to deep blacks. Patterns range from fairly regular graining and flecks to the exquisitely artistic veins that run through high-grade marble.

Stone floors are right at home in entryways, kitchens, and bathrooms, but the right stone works in other rooms as well. Oversized slate tiles or slabs in subtle dark hues look impressive in a contemporary living room. Travertine or sandstone brings a special panache to a modern

A bathroom is the ideal room to show off marble's spectacular look, because the small surface area limits the bill for what is one of the most expensive stones. This bathroom was designed with marble floor and walls, and the look spells luxury and opulence.

bedroom. Where the weather turns bitter cold, a stone floor can be installed over an under-floor heating system.

LAMINATE

Modern laminate flooring is durable, easy to install, and relatively water-resistant. It's made of a wood-and-resin foundation covered with a photographic layer underneath a protective topcoat. Manufacturers use the photographic layer to imitate just about any surface, from wood to stone and even ceramic tile. The protective topcoat resists moisture, which makes laminate great for bathrooms and kitchens. The best thing about laminates is that they are installed as *floating* floors—you don't need to nail them down or glue them to the subfloor. Just click them together in place, cutting where necessary to fit. As remarkable as the photographic layer technology is, you still shouldn't expect the variations in pattern and color you would see across the surface of a real wood, stone, or ceramic floor.

A "floating" laminate plank floor like this is easy to install and provides a soft surface to go along with a dark wood glow.

VINYL

Vinyl is some of the most popular flooring. That's because it's durable, is comfortable to walk on, and can be created in every color of the rainbow and with patterns from plain to fancy. Vinyl flooring is even produced in textured styles that impersonate the look of stone or ceramic tiles. Pick sheet vinyl for an unbroken waterproof floor surface, or choose the easier-to-install vinyl tiles. Either way, the cost is relatively low. However, some environmentalists balk at vinyl because the production and disposal of vinyl floors creates toxic byproducts. You should also vent any space where new vinyl flooring has been installed, because the flooring gives off irritating vapors.

Capturing the look and textured surface of a genuine mosaic stone tile floor, this sheet vinyl surface is easier to install, less expensive, and just as beautiful to the eye.

LINOLEUM AND MARMOLEUM

Linoleum—and its modern version, Marmoleum— is manufactured of all natural ingredients, including linseed oil, wood dust, pine rosin, and mineral fillers. The flooring is hypoallergenic, is antibacterial, and does not release noxious vapors. All that makes linoleum or Marmoleum pretty perfect for any home with small children and pets. These materials are also durable, soft, and warm to walk on. The color runs all the way through, so scratches are easy to fix. The available array of colors and patterns is astonishing. Choose from bold, solid colors; styles that look like wood or stone; or a boatload of patterns, from bold and brassy (like me!) to restrained and elegant (like me, too!). I've even seen linoleum that looks exactly like polished concrete (but is whole lot kinder to your soles).

Sheet linoleum is laid the old-fashioned way, cut to fit and glued to the subfloor. Laying linoleum tiles is something anyone can do. Even better, Marmoleum "click" planks snap together. Just keep in mind that tiles or planks are not watertight like a sheet floor would be.

CORK

Cork is a renewable tree bark and an environmentally friendly material. It has a truly one-of-kind appearance and a slightly spongy feel as you walk

Cork makes an ideal floor in this high-traffic kitchen. Durable and low-maintenance, this floor features an eye-catching pattern of cream and dark brown tiles.

on it. Cork's natural appearance runs from light brown to medium mocha, with mesmerizing grain patterns ranging from swirls to speckles. Depending on how the floor is finished, the color may darken naturally over time. Cork can be stained or colored, and is available as glue-down tiles or easier click-together planks. It's a simple-to-install, antistatic, hypoallergenic floor for a reasonable price.

CARPET

Just so we're clear: For the purposes of this discussion, *carpeting* is permanently installed wall-to-wall flooring, and *rugs* are loose, portable floor coverings. Carpet is made with one of five types of fiber:

- Wool is the only natural carpeting material, and it has a soft, silky feel (what pros call the hand). It is somewhat flame-retardant and naturally stain-resistant, but more prone to fading, and pricey.

- Nylon is a premium synthetic fiber with a lovely feel, good crush resistance, decent stain resistance, and reasonable colorfastness.

- Polyester feels as nice as nylon but is less durable.

- Triexta is a new type of polymer fiber that is made partially of corn byproducts; many consider it to be the fiber of the future. It combines softness with fade resistance and cleanability that rival or exceed nylon and polyester.

- Polypropylene (formerly olefin) is at the bottom of the quality—and price—range . This fiber is durable, water-resistant, fade-proof, and stain-resistant. It has the roughest feel and is the least crush-resistant.

Bedrooms are prime real estate for carpet coverage. A low-pile carpet such as this is lovely on bare feet. The subtle design adds a bit of understated flair to a soft, comfortable surface.

A living room floor has to hold up to traffic and still look good over time. So the choice of low, loop-pile nylon carpet was ideal for this room, and the understated color ensures that the carpet doesn't look dated in a year or two.

No matter which material you are drawn to, your wallet will have something to say about the choice because the type of fiber largely determines the carpet's price.

Pile describes how the fibers are used in the carpet. Some are looped, while others are cut to stand straight up. Looped fibers are more resistant and durable; cut pile is softer and nicer to walk on. The two are sometimes combined to create random or specific patterns in the carpet's surface. In high-traffic areas, choose a carpet with shorter fibers, a higher fiber count, or specially twisted fibers that resist crushing.

You'll hear confusing terms like *saxony* and *plush,* but the point is to find the carpet that serves your needs. Here's what I would suggest: Once you've settled on wall-to-wall carpeting, start with your budget. Economic reality is bound to eliminate an option or two. Then shop for styles at a large home center or carpet store (save money by purchasing remnants at carpet outlets). Retail suppliers display well-organized racks of carpet samples to help you assess the feel and see the actual color. Turn to the carpet warranty as an excellent indicator of how a specific carpet will hold up over time.

Lastly, carpets can affect indoor air quality. The typical new-carpet smell is actually an airborne volatile organic compound (VOC). Air carpet out for at least 24 hours before using room, or look for low-VOC carpets; they have an icon on the label showing that they've passed air-quality tests by the Carpet and Rug Institute's (CRI) Indoor Air Quality testing program.

You know you have the right carpet when it looks like it was made for the room. This brown floor covering blends in perfectly to the design's color scheme and complements the other textures in the room.

sabrina's tip

CARPET, ONE TILE AT A TIME

Back in the day, carpet tiles were tacky squares of substandard quality material, used by college kids to cover cold, bare dorm floors at a minimal cost. No more. Today, you can buy chic carpet squares in loads of styles and prints. These tiles can even be made with photographic images on the surface— something you won't find in wall-to-wall carpeting. I use them in place of area rugs to create unique patterns and sizes or unusual color combinations. The tiles could not be easier to install; they are usually stuck to the floor with adhesive pads or double-sided tape supplied by the manufacturer. This means that they can be rearranged as the mood strikes, or taken with you when you move.

choosing a flooring material

That's a passel of flooring options. Some will be out of your price range, which pares down the list. However, even within a given material such as wood, prices span a big divide. Don't forget your own creativity as well. For instance, rather than replace a floor with stunning teak, you can use oak for the field of the floor, with a linear teak border. It's a great way to exploit the beauty of a high-cost material in an extremely visible way.

I tend to be careful with carpeting. Colored carpeting can look dated rather quickly. Depending on the type of carpet, fading may be an issue— something that can become painfully clear when it comes time to rearrange the furniture in the room. Those reservations aside, I have to admit that a lush, carpeted floor can be a real treat for the feet in a bedroom or living room.

Laminate is a lower-cost alternative to wood, stone, or tile. Laminate manufacturers have

become proficient at mimicking the look of the actual materials. Even so, a laminate floor can't rival the appearance of something like an exotic hardwood or true Carrara marble. Laminate can, however, reliably stand in for basic oak strip flooring or brown or gray slate tiles. Your feet will thank you for the soft, warm surface.

When you simply must have the real thing, whether it's hardwood, ceramic tile, or stone, I say live with it before you buy. Take home samples, even if you have to purchase them. Judge the material against your other design elements. Think about the maintenance it requires. For instance, carpeting should be deep-cleaned once a year—twice if the floor sees heavy traffic, or if your kids and pets spend a lot of time there. Real wood floors need to be cleaned regularly to maintain their finish, and stone surfaces have their own upkeep.

Dining rooms are ideal spaces for laminates, which provide all the beauty of stone or wood, but in a warm, soft surface that's easy to clean and more forgiving of dropped stemware and plates.

If you're wondering why I haven't included rugs, it's because I think of rugs (even large ones) as floor coverings, not actual flooring. I use them to moderate the effect of floor color or pattern or the general look of the room design. In that sense, they come after the choice of flooring in the development of your design, so you'll find a discussion of rugs in *The Sixth Layer: Picking Your Textiles.*

Once you've sorted through the options and settled on the perfect flooring for your space, it's time to work your way up with wall surface treatments.

wonderful walls (including the one overhead)

Walls offer some of the richest design potential of any architectural feature in your home. Walls can be background to furniture or can serve as art in and of themselves. Create softly colored physical borders or richly textured facades that invite the hands as well as the eyes. Don't forget the ceiling. You'll hear designers refer to it as the "Fifth Wall." We call it that because it represents a ripe opportunity for some interesting decorative treatments. Let's start with the most popular wall (and ceiling) coating of all: paint.

Adding beadboard and deep cove molding to the tray ceiling in this well-appointed kitchen was an easy way to spice up the look overhead. Those same elements would work just as well on a flat ceiling.

a perfectly painted wall

Is it any wonder that paint is the most popular wall treatment? Painting a wall is instant gratification, and the potential looks are virtually limitless. Even if you stick with a basic solid-colored eggshell paint, you'll choose from a mind-boggling palette of colors. A simple coat of paint revitalizes and re-energizes the look of a room, but the design potential goes much, much further than that.

Painting a wall is instant gratification.

You've probably seen walls done in one of the many special painting techniques that include sponging, rag-rolling, stippling, brushing, and combing. (Sounds like a long Sunday afternoon at the spa!) These techniques are easy to do,

which is why they have been a little overused. A one-of-a-kind effect isn't so special when it's used in every house on the block. It's also easy to miss the mark. Rag-rolling a wall isn't hard, but work with the wrong colors and the result will be regrettable.

sabrina's tip

PAINT HEALTHY

Modern technology is amazing. The quality of water-based latex paints has caught up to once-far-superior, oil-based alkyd paints. Interior paints dry quicker than ever, with far less fumes. But just because you can't smell a paint doesn't make it safe. To protect indoor air quality, especially in a home where children or seniors live, I use low-VOC (volatile organic compound) or no-VOC paints. They cost a little more, but I think the peace of mind is well worth the added expense.

sabrina's tip

DECAL YOUR WALL

Looking for a cool wall decoration somewhere between a plain painted surface and wallpaper? I've got just the thing for you: temporary wall decals. Decal companies offer many designs from witty to whimsical. You can even order custom designs.

You'll find the biggest selection of wall decals online, but no matter where you buy them, they're easy to put up. Just measure, mark the orientation, peel off a backing so that the adhesive side is exposed, and stick it carefully to the wall. Smooth out the decal, and you've got a brand-new wall decoration in minutes. They can be removed when you want to change the look or you move to a new place, but in any case, they're not really right in traditional decors. As interesting as these are, I would limit them to a child's or teen's bedroom, a very casual space or in a pantry.

Fact is, less is more when it comes to special painting techniques. Stippled gray walls in a powder room, with undertones of off-white or muted yellow, create intriguing visual depth. An entire glazed living room or a completely rag-rolled bedroom can be hard to pull off and will usually be a bit much.

Sheen is another factor that will figure into your paint selection. There are four basic paint sheens that determine how shiny the surface will be when the paint dries. These include flat, eggshell or satin (manufacturers use these terms interchangeably), semi-gloss, and high gloss. Generally, the glossier the finish the easier it is to clean, and the more it will show surface imperfections.

When you're selecting a paint finish, remember that the shinier the finish, the more difficult it is to touch-up without seeing a difference in sheen.

- **Flat/matte:** Use flat for low-traffic rooms, on walls that are perfectly smooth, and where you want a true representation of the paint color. This finish is my number one choice for bedrooms, living rooms, and dining rooms. Although it is very easy to touch up, flat paint is not easy to clean unless you purchase a high-end brand of paint.
- **Eggshell/Satin:** If you want a small amount of sheen, use eggshell or satin in rooms that see medium to high traffic or where you want to amplify light. Satin is a great paint for children's bedrooms, laundry rooms, family rooms, kitchens, and bathrooms because it has a scrubbable finish.
- **Semi-gloss:** Turn to semi-gloss for trim, moldings, and interior doors. Because of its resistance to humid conditions, it can be used in kitchens and bathrooms.
- **High gloss:** Although it is extremely durable, only use this paint if your surface is very smooth because all the imperfections will become visible. Save high gloss for cabinetry, main entry doors, or casework and ornate molding in formal, sophisticated interiors where you just want these details to pop. Keep in mind that the shinier the finish, the more light will be reflected

around the room. Colors under glossier surfaces will appear lighter and less intense, and less rich than under a matte surface.

For all its allure, paint may not do it for you. That's okay. Where you're yearning for something a bit different, you have a lot of other wall-surfacing options to choose from.

winning wallcoverings

Wallcoverings are all about pattern and texture, two of the most intriguing interior design elements. Wallpaper designs can captivate the eye, and a surface like grass cloth just begs to be touched. Other wallcoverings combine the visual and tactile in one neat material. Shop around and

you'll find subtle types, like monochromatic linen, and more outrageous alternatives, such as foil wallpaper in a pop-art color scheme. That's part of the magic of wallcoverings—there's one for every taste and any room.

- **Paper, vinyl, and beyond.** Uncoated wallpaper (sometimes called *English paper*) is fragile stuff that takes special skills to install. It's a high-end material, elegant and formal, and meant for rooms and walls that won't see much wear and tear. Coated paper, paper-backed vinyl, and solid vinyl wallpaper are more practical and affordable. Coated papers resist dirt and moisture to a modest degree and work well in bedrooms, hallways, and living rooms. Where bathrooms or kitchens are concerned, however, a vinyl paper is almost a

This stunningly sophisticated striped wallpaper features a chocolate brown and beige combination that perfectly complements the room's blue and brown color scheme. The look of the walls does justice to the high-style furnishings and, as a bonus, makes the room look bigger.

A rich, horizontally striped pattern gives this bathroom a more spacious feeling, and adds a great deal of visual interest. The wallpaper is vinyl, resistant to moisture and easy to clean.

Wallpaper provides the option of adding incredible patterns to a room design. The paper in this bedroom features a large-scale pattern most appropriate for a larger room or area.

necessity. Vinyl wallpapers hang tough in the face of moisture and even grease splatters, and clean up with relative ease. Paper-backed vinyls are tougher and more durable, but you can judge how hardy any wallpaper will be by checking its label. "Washable" or "cleanable" means that the surface can tolerate a kid's room. "Scrubbable" describes a paper that can hold up to a busy kitchen atmosphere.

Textured papers have a raised design that helps hide wall imperfections and is paintable. *Foils* are wallpapers made of metallic foil layered on a paper base. Most are shiny, although the surface can be matte or satin as well. Foils reflect light, making them ideal for darker rooms. Colors tend to pop under the shiny finish, but grays and more muted colors take on an enchanting character rendered in foil. Foils are, however, a little tough to work with, can present hot spots or glare in a bright room or where a light bulb is partially exposed, and the surface will magnify wall imperfections. I would use a foil paper in smaller spaces such as entry halls, where they can provide a visual charge to a confined space.

- Fabrics. Textiles have been used throughout history to cover walls, from palaces to bungalows. Fabric wallcoverings are luxurious, and each has its own inviting texture, from the elegant irregularity of raw silk and linen, to the engaging woven look of sisal and raffia, to the nearly liquid sheen of chintz or high-gloss synthetics such as polyester or olefin. Walls covered in fabric are undeniably gorgeous, but they are also inevitably delicate and expensive. I use them in low-traffic rooms, such as guest bedrooms and formal dining rooms.

- The naturals. Grass cloth is the most popular of this group, but there are many interesting natural wallcoverings. I've used wood bark and wood veneer mounted on a fiber backing to create intriguing walls. Bamboo papers look like a cross between fiber and fabric and come in several different stains and shades.

new surface, new space

Wallcovering patterns and shades can affect how we perceive physical dimensions. Wallpaper with vertical stripes makes a ceiling seem higher. Natural wallcoverings with weaves or grains that run vertically create the same effect. Careful, though: If walls, windows, or doorways are even slightly out of plumb (not square), vertical stripes or lines will magnify the imperfections. Always check your walls and wall openings for square when you're considering a wallcovering with a strong vertical design. Pattern matters, too. Make a room look larger with big wallpaper patterns; make it appear cozier and more intimate with busy, small patterns.

Anytime you're leaning toward a wallcovering with a busy pattern, jump ahead a few layers and think about wall-mounted art (see page 168), storage (see page 81), and furniture (see page 105) that will be visually set against the wall. Busy patterns are ripe for visual conflicts, so it's good to think through the rest of the elements in the space to make sure you don't go to all the trouble of putting up a spectacular floral fabric wallpaper only to find that it clashes with everything else in the room.

detailing wall surfaces

Let's not stop at one-dimensional wall decoration. As lovely as paint and wallcoverings can be, moldings, trim, and casework are unique and arresting decorative details. They are easy to add, enhance, or change.

Molding is a prime example. Contemporary interiors often lack crown molding (molding that covers the seam between walls and ceiling) and include only the most modest baseboard molding. You can transform the look of a room by adding detailed molding along the ceiling seams, or new casework around a door or window. Once made of plaster, stone, or wood, molding faces, or *profiles,* were limited in detail. Modern synthetic moldings can be made in any size or shape. You'll find wide

and incredibly detailed historical molding profiles, or combine simple and straight molding pieces for your own signature look. Polyurethane moldings are usually produced in bright white, but can be painted any color you want.

> Modern synthetic moldings can be made in any size or shape.

The more intricate and elaborate the molding profile, the more formal the look. Curving flourishes are associated with an ornate interior style, one that might include floral wallpaper, period furniture, and ornate accents. A simpler or more geometric style will suit a wider range of decors. Simple, linear moldings complement furniture with simple lines, uncomplicated textile patterns, solid colors, and modest accents.

I'm a big believer in using the same molding treatments throughout the house. Different molding treatments used in different rooms breaks up visual continuity. This puts a lot more weight on any decision you make about moldings or trim because it might mean running crown molding throughout several rooms. However, other types of wall ornamentation can be used in a single room. Chair rails—horizontal moldings placed about a third of the way up the wall and used to stop chairs from bumping into the wall—are perfect for dressing up dining room or kitchen walls. Picture rails run horizontally along a wall a foot or two below the top and can serve as decorative elements in just about any room other than a bathroom. They can also be used to hang photos or art without driving nails into the wall. Picture rails also moderate the effect of high ceilings, giving the room a better sense of visual proportion. You can even use decorative moldings to create shapes and patterns in the middle of a wall.

Captivating wall color combines with bright white linear wall moldings and chair rails to create an enchanting hallway look. You can easily re-create a look like this using aftermarket synthetic moldings.

the well-dressed wall

If you're willing to go beyond simple moldings, you might want to clad a wall in a whole new surface. A new surface such as wood or metal makes any wall a focal point and rarely needs to be used on every wall in the room.

WAINSCOTING

Formed of boards or panels positioned from the bottom of the wall to anywhere between waist and shoulder height, today's wainscoting is as much a decorative element as it is wall protection. Accent your cottage dining room wit wainscot panels formed from tongue-and-groove pine boards. Add a graceful touch to any decor with beadboard wainscoting. Perk up a country kitchen with tin sheet versions. Use distinctive molding to border the top of the wall, or separate individual panels and create your own signature look. Stain or paint the molding to work with the room's design. I especially like those treatments in busy foyers, social kitchens, and formal dining rooms.

Wainscoting, like ornate molding, is often painted bright white, especially where dark or bold colors might overwhelm. The dark wall color in this bathroom might have closed in the space, but instead, the room looks fresh and bright with the help of the wainscot.

WOOD PANELING

Real wood paneling is handsome, cozy, and warm; it has a rich, interesting look in contrast to the fake product widely used in suburban homes through the '50s, '60s, and '70s. Create a rugged wall perfect for a farmhouse interior out of wide, rough-sawn planks. Go for a more refined appearance with smooth, narrow tongue-and-groove boards. You can even panel a wall with wide, tall sheets of high-grade oak, birch, or other plywood to create broad, flat sections full of scintillating grain pattern. Play with the look by varying the direction of the boards.

Straight up and down is traditional, but boards run diagonally give an informal and interesting appearance. Horizontal paneling is an unexpected sight, appropriate for a wall in a modern or contemporary interior.

The finish is a big part of a paneled wall. High-quality woods deserve to be finished natural. Stain paneling if you like, but I find that painting it runs counter to a big reason for choosing it in the first place—the beauty and warmth of the wood.

Wood-paneled walls make for a distinctively dramatic look in a bathroom. Raised rails and stiles add to a look that is entirely sophisticated.

sabrina's tip

THE TAO OF TIN

A few years ago, I had a client who wanted a unique backsplash for her all-white English cottage kitchen. I found copper-plated tin-ceiling panels and installed them to create a truly distinctive wall surface. The client absolutely loved the look. Tin-ceiling suppliers copy dozens of antique designs and offer just as many new patterns. You can buy the panels with tin, copper, or brass surfaces plated over a more durable base metal, and they are easy as pie to put up. The finish options— and the fact that you can paint the surface—give you lots of leeway in customizing the look. I like tin as a backsplash, but it also works as wainscoting and, of course, as a stunning ceiling.

METAL

Metal may seem like a cold choice for a wall surface, but don't discount metals out of hand. Imagine an accent wall covered in hammered copper partnered with a warm color scheme and wood furniture. Surface a backsplash in a gourmet kitchen with stainless steel and you reinforce the notion of serious cooking. Personally, I like the look of a metal wall surface in sleek, contemporary spaces or modern interiors, although there's no reason that a rough copper wall or rusted iron plates couldn't be used to add a bit of zest to a farmhouse interior.

STONE

Accentuate a ho-hum fireplace with a floor-to-ceiling column of stacked flagstone, or use it to build a distinctive low divider wall. Irregular stones make for a casual look, while cut stone is a more formal style. Give your living room a Tuscan feel with a long wall covered in a veneer that looks like stacked fieldstone. Use synthetic solid-surface veneers textured and colored to look like granite or marble as the perfect walls for a bathroom.

Stunning Ming green marble mosaic tile in irregular shapes creates an incredible backdrop for his-and-her sinks in a modern bathroom. A wall of stone can be one of the most captivating surfaces in a room.

A fireplace surround covered with travertine mosaic tile interspersed with glass tiles will surely compete with the fire for attention. It's a crisp, contemporary look.

VERTICAL TILE

When it comes to adding interest to a wall surface, it's hard to top a tiled wall. However, with few exceptions, tiled walls are limited to the kitchen and bath. Much of what I've already covered about tiled floors holds true for walls. You can use the same types of tiles on both surfaces, and the basic principles—such as dressing up a plain white tile field with a

border of hand-painted tiles—works for walls as well.

The big difference between the two surfaces is that floors often look best covered by larger tiles, while walls are usually covered with smaller tiles, or similar sizes in different shapes. That's not to say that you can't use travertine tiles on the wall around the spa tub in your master bath, but the larger the tile, the more gravity wants to pull it down. Some shapes and sizes, such as rectangular subway tiles and bull-nose finish tiles, are pretty much exclusive to walls.

Take your color and pattern cues for tiled walls from a tiled floor. Use checkerboard patterns or different tile directions to make a wall stand out, or use details such as a section of colored or specialty tiles. Backsplashes are the exception. I look at these small areas as places to use tile and tile designs that diverge from what was done on a floor or countertop. The actual surface area is modest, so splurging on more expensive tiles usually isn't going to set back your budget. For instance, a tiled mural would perfectly accent a Mediterranean-style kitchen and could serve as a sensational focal point all by itself.

Some of the most common applications for glass tiles are kitchen backsplashes. This eye-catching surface is exceptional for the glass tiles, and the interesting shapes that give the design a horizontal flow.

a bit of style overhead

I can't tell you the number of homeowners I've come across who simply never look up when considering a room design. It's a shame. Certainly, not every room calls for a ceiling surface treatment, but it's worth considering. Walk into a space with exposed beams or a tray ceiling and you'll see what I mean.

Create the illusion of architectural elements for an impressive look. The appearance of exposed beams can be created with hollow, U-shaped, plastic channels attached at intervals suggesting the real thing. Dramatic and eye-catching, they work best in a formal interior.

Ceilings can also be paneled. Tongue-and-groove boards are a traditional look, while shiplapped or butt-joined planks create a more informal appearance. Panel boards always look better on an angled ceiling such as a cathedral ceiling. Flat ceilings often look better decorated by square wood panels bordered with molding—a formal and powerful look.

Make a less expensive design statement with faux plaster medallions and moldings. Traditional ceiling plasterwork requires master craftsmanship, but the same high style is within reach with the help of lightweight synthetic reproductions of medallions, moldings, and surface ornamentations. Once installed, these are virtually indistinguishable from genuine plasterwork. Again, even plain medallions are a fairly formal look.

choose the right wall treatment

The type of wall decoration you use should give a nod to your design goals, fit comfortably in your budget, and appeal to your tastes. Wainscoting wows in a formal dining room, but if your wallet says it's either the wainscoting or a crucial piece of furniture, make do with painted walls.

sabrina's tip

GLASS TILE WALLS

There's something incredibly sensual and tactile about glass tiles. Sometimes used on floors, they stand out most when covering walls or countertops. The glass is colored all the way through, and the color will never fade. Because they are fairly translucent, the tiles are backed with white latex. This not only prevents the mounting surface and adhesive from showing through the tile, but also makes the colors really pop. The tiles are offered in an impressive palette of colors and are installed in the same way as ceramic tiles. A glass tile surface is also easy to clean and won't stain, making glass tile an ideal choice for a bathroom shower surround or kitchen backsplash.

An incredible paneled ceiling with exposed beams adds a ton of drama to this living room. Using the treatment on a regular height has to be done with caution, however, because the look visually lowers to the ceiling.

Well-known for bold colors that seem lit from within, glass tiles can also be used for a subtle and understated look, as evidence by this kitchen wall.

Practical issues will affect your choice as well. Older homes can shift over time, skewing doorways and windows. If your walls are noticeably showing their age, choose surface treatments that will disguise imperfections. Thick vinyl wallpaper, dark paint, and paneling are all good at hiding less-than-perfect walls. Reflective surfaces, tiles, and thin coatings such as foil highlight unsightly or irregular walls.

chic countertops

Talk about countertops and you're really talking about two rooms—the kitchen and the bathroom. Countertops in either room have to handle the

A stunning kitchen often starts with stunning countertops. This room is no exception, and features two different types of quartz countertops. Quartz features all the beauty of granite, with many additional benefits.

presence of water, and they need to be easy to clean. Regardless, you want your counters to look sharp. Advances in synthetic materials and new technologies give us an ever-expanding menu of countertop options. You will have no problem finding a countertop material that perfectly suits your style and your budget.

I like to mix countertop materials, using a different material on the island than the main counters (I'll also mix cabinet styles that way). It's a great way to make an island seem unique and to personalize the kitchen design.

ceramic tile

The standard kitchen and bathroom countertop choice, ceramic tile, is available in just about every color imaginable and priced from high to low. A properly tiled counter is easy to clean and resists moisture. My hesitation in choosing

ceramic tile for a countertop is the issue of grout lines. Grout lines inevitably degrade. Left untreated, they collect dirt, grime, and food particles. Though, it's a pretty modest problem that is easy to fix. Home centers and hardware stores offer cleaners developed specifically to deal with this problem, and you can seal grout. You can also turn to colored grout to create the appearance of a continuous surface.

sabrina's tip

COUNTERTOP LUXURY AT A DISCOUNT

Want the look of granite without the hefty price? Turn to granite overlay countertops. These are basically shells of granite that are crafted to your measurements and then installed right over, and glued to, your existing countertops.

Granite overlay countertops convincingly mimic the look—and durability—of a solid-stone surface, with a big savings in cost.

Engineered-stone countertops come in many different natural appearances, but they can also be manufactured in just about any color—including vibrant hues like this bright green.

Because they include actual stone, engineered-stone surfaces capture much of the beauty of quarried stone products, with even more durability and less maintenance.

stone

Stone countertops are all about opulence. The same quarry stone available as flooring is offered as countertops. They aren't cheap, but you'll be buying a surface that will give you decades of use.

- **Granite** is the most popular choice for countertops, largely because it comes in beautiful, rich colors from black to pink to bluish gray. You can set hot cookware on a granite countertop without worry, and the surface is scratch-resistant as well. Granite is usually polished to an attractive shine.

- **Marble** countertops are stunning. When you spend a little more, you can shop the magnificent world of marble. However, you should know that this beautiful stone can easily become stained and marred unless the surface is sealed regularly. Marble ranges from white to black and every color in between, but it's the magnificent veining that makes this material so intriguing.

- **Slate** is durable and easy to maintain. Scratches can be buffed out, and the surface can be revived with a quick wipe-down of mineral oil. Slate comes in fewer colors than granite and marble—usually limited to grays, blacks, and greens—and the surface is generally left in its natural matte finish (although slate can be polished to a high gloss).

- **Soapstone** is a less expensive alternative that comes in black, beige, and gray, with fine spidery lines of white spreading across the surface. It's a softer stone and is sold with either a polished or an unpolished (honed) surface. Unlike marble, soapstone is warm to the touch.

- **Limestone** has an elegant look, with delicate veins and muted colors from rose to light black. Limestone countertops are usually honed rather than polished, creating a more durable and textured surface. Just the same, limestone is more susceptible to scratches, cracks, and staining than other quarry stones.

engineered stone

The magic of science is to improve on nature, and that's the goal of the companies that develop and produce engineered-stone countertops. These countertops are crafted from a blend of more than 90 percent crushed quartz with a small amount of binders such as resins. The combination is harder and more durable than natural quarry stone. Engineered stone is highly resistant to scratches, stains, and burn marks, and the surface requires no maintenance other than regular cleaning. The countertops are available in dozens of colors, all with a simple, regular pattern or larger flecks. An engineered-stone countertop won't feature the extreme vein patterns of marble or the subtle color variations of high-end granite, but it does come in either a polished or a matte surface.

concrete

Concrete isn't just the stuff of sidewalks anymore. The surface is commonly polished smooth to repel moisture and prevent stains, but a high-gloss finish also adds life and visual depth to the solid gray color. However, you don't have to settle for gray. Concrete can be tinted in lots of colors, and the

material can be easily formed to just about any shape. The counter can be poured offsite and then polished and installed (the most common method), or the forms can be built at your location and the counters poured right in place. Either way, you'll wind up with a durable, hip surface with a seriously unique look. That look is most appropriate to high-tech, modern, or streamlined contemporary kitchens. You should also keep in mind that depending on what material was used in your cabinets and how they were constructed, the weight of the countertop may require reinforcing the cabinets.

solid surface

When it comes to countertops, *solid surface* means synthetic formulations that create seamless counters. High-quality solid-surface countertops

It's hard to top a concrete countertop. Durable and industrial, this unfinished surface would fit in with a modern kitchen.

are very durable and won't stain or fade. They are not, however, as hard as natural stone, and they are susceptible to scratching and burning if exposed to knives or high heat. These countertops are popular largely because they are formed as

Solid-surface countertops can be formed to just about any shape and can be manufactured in one piece with additional features, such as a backsplash.

one piece; there are no seams to catch dirt or visually break up the surface. Backsplashes and even sinks can be formed as one piece with the countertop. Because manufacturers control the production process, they offer a full complement of colors and even grains, flecks, and vein patterns. Most homeowners choose a satin finish, although solid-surface countertops are offered in semi-gloss and high-gloss finishes as well.

wood

Perhaps not as popular as they were in the heyday of butcher block, wood countertops are still a reasonable option. Many different species are available, including predictable standards such as oak and surprising exotics such as zebrawood. Most can be stained to suit your design needs and preferences, and the surface is sealed with a food-safe, organic penetrating oil that prevents water infiltration and staining.

Wood countertops don't have to be used throughout the kitchen to be an effective design element. The top of this island is an eye-catching accent in the room.

Being wood, the counters are vulnerable to scratching, but some would say that a few scars here and there just add to the character of the material.

metal

I'm not a huge fan of metal countertops, but that's not to say they don't have a place in the right kitchen. Whether it's stainless steel or the less common copper, metal counters point to a professional cook's kitchen. The surfaces are sleek and stylish, best suited to more modern kitchens or more subdued designs, such as an all-white kitchen. The price can be far lower than other countertops, and there's virtually no maintenance. Keeping a metal countertop clean can be a challenge, however, as anyone who owns stainless-steel appliances can attest. The

surface tends to spot or streak unless you use special cleansers.

recycled glass

Feeling green? Channel your inner environmentalist by shopping for countertops made out of recycled glass. Among the most popular is the version known by the pre-eminent brand name Vetrazzo. These mix fragments of glass into a concrete substrate to form fascinating surfaces. The manufacturer recycles glass from a variety of sources, which means that the countertops come in lots of colors and color combinations (although the bonding medium is always the same grayish-white). Like concrete countertops, Vetrazzo surfaces can be manufactured to particular and unique specs, such as curving countertops.

Stainless-steel countertops make for a sharp look in this kitchen. The cold surface contrasts with the warmth of the eucalyptus end-grain breakfast bar counter. Combining natural materials like this often leads to a winning look.

Recycled glass countertops can be a sophisticated look—the perfect complement to other design elements in a contemporary kitchen. Although vivid colors are available, more low-key countertops such as this white product suit a wider range of design styles.

These countertops may look exactly like slate, but they are actually high-quality laminate installed for far less than genuine stone would have cost.

laminate

Laminate countertops are some of the most economical choices for homeowners looking to redo bathrooms or kitchens on a tight budget. Laminates were once low-quality surfaces with exposed seams that would capture dirt and food particles, but today's products are higher quality. The countertops are created by bonding a thin sheet of acrylic to a base of particleboard or other wood substrate. Modern laminates are available in a variety of colors and patterns, and many include decorative edging such as bevels. The surface won't stain and it resists moisture— although standing liquids can infiltrate the seams. Laminate countertops can be damaged by hot cookware and are susceptible to scratching, but they clean up easily and require virtually no maintenance.

Whether you're outfitting a kitchen with beautiful countertops or papering a bedroom wall with a retro vinyl design that you found online, decorating interior surfaces is a surprisingly fun step in your great design adventure. Having made the decisions about what to do with your surfaces, it's time to jump to the next layer and plan your clutter-killing storage strategies.

integrate storage to organize your space

call this the hodgepodge layer because your storage solutions are going to edge into a lot of other design layers, including furniture, wall surfaces, and accents. Don't get too caught up in that. I'll cover a lot of ground here, but keep in mind that the ultimate goal is to integrate storage solutions that perfectly meet your needs and add to the design in every instance. To paraphrase an old saying, "A stunning place for everything, and everything in its stunning place."

Creating appropriately designed-in storage solutions begins with a clear-headed assessment of what you need to store. I only add storage and organizers that address particular—rather than vague and general—needs. I also position storage as close as possible to where it will be used. A laundry hamper in the bedroom isn't going to be as effective as one placed in the bathroom, if that is where you undress.

Focus on the specific kind of clutter that plagues the room you're designing. Options and answers will often pop right out at you. Is your well-used family room an obstacle course of toys? Then you'll need a solution(s) that not only efficiently stores all the sizes and shapes of your children's toys, but also is accessible and easy for your children to use. The simpler it is for them to put away the toys, the more likely it is that they'll get in the habit of picking them up. (That philosophy works equally well for teenagers, husbands, and houseguests!)

Regardless of what you have to store, a measuring tape will be your number-one tool in determining your actual storage needs. A couple of years ago, I worked with a couple whose clutter had simply gotten the best of them. They were big readers, and a corner of their living room was literally overrun with books. The bookshelf was so overstuffed that the shelves were bowed. I suggested that they donate some of the books, but they told me that they loved their books and

wanted to keep them. Period. The husband said, "Let's just get another bookshelf." But that's not the way it works. I handed him a measuring tape and had him measure all their extra books to figure out the actual storage they needed. As it turned out, they needed *three* new bookshelves! Integrating the shelves seamlessly into the room design involved a lot of planning. Moral of the story: Measure before you make any storage decisions. That goes for clothing, toys, toiletries, and linens, too.

Armed with the right measurements, you can begin sorting through the many types of storage to find solutions that will best serve you and your design. In general, there are two ways to store things: exposed or hidden. I don't like to walk into a bathroom and see a bunch of toiletries on the counters or shelves. Storage units and organizers break down further into three specific types (most rooms benefit from a combination):

- "Reorganizers" that change what's there, like cabinet and closet systems
- Built-ins and add-ons, which include wall-mounted storage
- Stand-alone storage, which is either furniture meant specifically as storage or dual-purpose furnishings that contain hidden compartments

Previous page: I love to use shelves as complements to cabinetry in a kitchen. It's a natural: lots of easy-to-access space and the chance to display beautiful plates and stemware.

sabrina's rule

SHED BEFORE YOU STORE

When it comes to organizing a room, I don't wait for spring to launch into some serious spring cleaning. Starting fresh with a new room design means clearing out all those things you don't need or want anymore. I have clients sort everything into three groups: one for trash (such as broken toys); one for recycling or giving away (such as gym equipment you haven't used since you bought it); and a third for everything that will be kept. My clients are shocked to discover how much of their stuff they can do without. (If you haven't touched something in a year, you probably never will.) By paring down their belongings, they set the stage for a fresh start to go with the new room design. That's one of the best feelings of all.

The best bathroom vanities offer abundant storage. This wall-mounted unit not only offers a clean, sharp look, but it also provides plenty of hidden storage with spacious shelves just right for rolled-up towels and much more.

This small, modern living room features big-room storage in organized—and artistic—shelving. As a bonus, there is a fold-down guest bed concealed behind the white panel next to the orange shelves.

Shelving is the one type of storage solution that comes in all three styles and is appropriate for every room in the house. So let's talk shelving before we dive into specific solutions for each room in the house.

in the open, it can be put in a container . . . that can be put on a shelf. I'm not crazy for shelves just because they are a place to put just about anything. I'm crazy for them because they are the ideal storage solution and are available in all kinds of decorative styles.

shelving your way to order

Shelves are the Swiss Army knives of home organization. Most anything you need to put away can be put away on a shelf. If you don't want it out

standalone shelves

Take a quick look at the many types of free-standing shelving units and you'll see what I mean. In love with wood? You'll find a virtual forest of wood-shelving units, from chunky solid wood structures to basic units made of MDF (medium-density

The right shelf in the right place can serve as more than just a storage area. This simple unit features canted (angled) shelves that are just right for showing off a collection of vintage records. The bright white veneer of the storage unit pops out against the aqua wall.

fiberboard). Got a particular stain in mind? Shelves come in every shade from ebony to pickled. Metal more your style? Got you covered in stainless steel, anodized aluminum, iron, and plain bent steel. But let's not stop there. How about wire utility shelves for a utility room? Or maybe enamel-coated steel shelves to introduce a shock of color to a kid's room? I think you get the picture. There's a shelf for every taste and budget.

Before you select a shelving unit, though, you need to measure. You already know how much storage space you need. Now you need to determine where in the room a shelf unit that size will comfortably fit. Free-standing shelving units are most commonly placed up against a wall. Where you have plenty of wall space, you'll choose between horizontal and vertical shelving. Tall units can be great for storing things you want seen, like a set of leather-bound books. They have more visual power than lower, horizontal units, simply because they stand at eye level. Horizontal units, however, leave lots of wall space above them for art, mirrors, or other hangings, and the top of the unit can be used as a console table for lamps or to display small pictures.

Truly free-standing (backless) shelf units can also serve dual roles. A full-height backless unit can function as an engaging room divider. It's a terrific way to break up a long, narrow room or block off a cozy reading corner in a larger living room. Some shelving units are so uniquely designed that they provide a graphic focal point in a room—a real plus above and beyond their storage role.

wall-mounted shelves

Choose from the many different styles of wall-mounted shelves by picking a unit that provides all

Think of more than storage when shopping for shelf units. A simple and handsome backless cube shelf unit such as the one shown here makes a great side table. A larger version could serve as an excellent room divider.

the storage you need—including adequate support for heavier items—and fits into your design vision.

- **Floating.** The name comes from the fact that the shelf supports are hidden by the shelf. It's a cool look that seems to fit in anywhere, and suits any style. There are floating shelves in metal, dark and light woods, white and black melamine, and stylized versions with special edge treatments. They can handle a limited amount of weight—a row of thick, hard-bound books is probably out of the question. But a floating shelf can be great for keeping keys and glasses within reach in a foyer.

- **Bracket.** A basic shelf is set on two or more brackets that are screwed into a stud or into special anchors in sheetrock or plaster. The brackets are available in styles ranging from plain to spectacularly detailed. Brackets are usually used for only a single short shelf, although longer shelves can placed across three or four brackets.

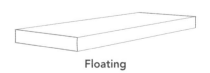

Floating

Bracket

- **Track and bracket.** Until a decade ago, this was a purely functional style in which shelf brackets were slotted into wall-mounted tracks. The tracks once looked fairly plain and utilitarian, but newer versions feature slick, modern styles in a variety of materials, interesting designs, and different finishes. Depending on the length of the track, several shelves can be stacked in a column. The beauty of the system is that shelf position is adjustable.

- **Vanity and towel.** These modest shelves are made specifically for bathrooms (although there's nothing preventing you from using them elsewhere as the need arises). The shelves are often glass, and the brackets are usually minimal and mounted right into the wall so that the shelf is fixed into the brackets rather than sitting on top of them. The unit is meant to be a minimal decorative element.

- **Cubes.** Wall-mounted cubes exploded onto the decorating scene about a decade ago and show no signs of going away. Nor should they; they're cool, useful, and available in a bunch of

styles and materials. The basic idea is the same no matter what type you choose—provide a solid surrounding surface that supports items that would be prone to falling off a flat shelf. You can use more than one to create fun decorative patterns on a wall. The look is informal, but it can work well in contemporary, modern, and eclectic interiors.

- **Wall units.** Choose a wall-mounted shelving unit where you need abundant shelf space but want to keep the floor free. These units contain multiple shelves in a box structure, which is screwed to the wall either through a solid back panel or through special mounting brackets on the back of the shelves. Wall-mounted shelving units are often painted the same color as the wall to prevent visual heaviness.

Shelves provide a ton of extremely adaptable and varied storage. I sometimes use identical small shelving units in different rooms to establish design continuity. Just the same, shelves alone can't do it all. To make sure that any room you

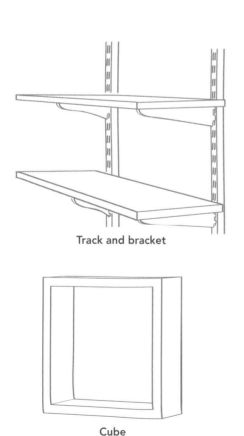

Track and bracket

Cube

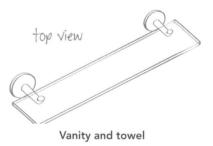

Vanity and towel

Wall unit

design stays organized and clutter-free, you're going need storage solutions tailored to the specific space you're designing.

imposing order in every room

Each room has its own clutter, which means that every room requires its own organizing strategies. Fortunately, you can tap into a wealth of over-the-counter room organizers and storage units. What you can't find at retail, you can create by turning to that ever-present resource—your own creativity.

an orderly entryway

It doesn't matter whether you have a grand entry hall or a tiny little postage stamp just inside the front door; the space is a transition area.

Transition invites clutter ("I'll just set it down for a second . . ."). That's why entryways should provide adequate seasonal storage for outer clothing and should have designated locations for all those little but important things that are so easily lost elsewhere in the house, like mail, keys, and eyeglasses.

I start organizing an entryway by providing a concealed place for footwear. It can't just be the floor by the door. Instead, lay out the modest expense for any one of the many shoe organizers sold at retail stores. I prefer designs that can be easily concealed in a closet or other area.

Next comes storage for outerwear. If there's no clear place to put a coat, it will inevitably get draped over furniture or, worse, dropped on the floor somewhere (it depends on the age of the coat wearer). There are three options for coat storage. Ideally, you have a closet with hangers. In the absence of a closet, turn to coat hooks or a free-standing coat rack—or a combination of

When it comes to making kitchens easy to work in, a mix of storage types is key. The shelves in this sleek modern room hold frequently used cooking gear for quick access. The variety of cabinet sizes and drawers ensures that gear of any shape or size can be accommodated.

A big family calls for big organization, especially in the main entryway. Here, large shelving units provide all the storage needed for a back-door mudroom entry. The storage is varied, accommodating many different shapes and sizes of items.

Storage solutions—like all the elements in your design—are best when they involve imagination. The homeowner in this house with no formal entry created plenty of entryway storage, with a simple and attractive set of cube shelves that line the steps of the stairs.

the two. Coat racks let you establish style in a very small footprint and are a great alternative to closet space. Pick a style that blends into the surrounding room design, or choose a unique look that stands out as a decorative accent. Not only does a rack hold coats, but many designs incorporate an umbrella stand in the base, or a shelf for shoes. That can be useful, but for maximum flexibility in where, and how many, coats or other outerwear you can organize, turn to hooks.

I go the extra mile to find hooks that have flair and that pick up on the prevailing design style. Even though they're small, hooks can be eye-grabbing accents. I've seen wonderful coat hooks adapted from old French faucet handles (chrome, with enameled white buttons showing the letters for hot and cold). Big, simple chrome hooks are perfect for a modern entry, while a row of wood pegs would better suit a country-style interior. Smaller hooks mounted by a door can be perfect for keeping keys where you can quickly find them as you head out. However they're used, hooks are a simple and inexpensive way to get organize and be creative.

Mail accounts for a lot of entryway clutter, which is why I use a specific container such as a woven basket or lacquered tray for incoming mail. Providing simple and functional short-term "spot" storage like this not only keeps a room organized, it makes life easier because everyone in the house knows specifically where things go.

Sometimes the formal front entry sees less use than a more convenient side or back door. I like to expand the storage in an informal entryway, such as a mudroom, by including the same features you would in an entryway—for coats, keys, and shoes—with extra storage for things like sporting goods and large, flat surfaces for grocery bags and other transitional items. The best multipurpose storage I've come across for mudrooms are cubby shelves that include a row of hooks underneath a series of cavities that can be assigned to different members of the household.

A simple row of hooks serves almost any entryway well.

Organizing a large common space such a living room or family room can be a major challenge. Common spaces are gathering areas for clutter as well as people. That's why the space calls for a multitude of storage strategies.

- **Master the media.** The potential clutter from electronics includes CDs, DVDs, and video games. You can place all that stuff out in the open on living room shelving. Personally, though, I find that these items are not very attractive in their own right. My preference is always to transfer what's on CDs and DVDs to computer. Barring that, I hide them away in a row of boxes—in my living room's accent color—on a shelf unit next to my home theater system. However, if you're okay with the look of the packaging, you'll find a lot of dedicated wall-mounted units designed to store CDs and DVDs. I'm not a real big fan of this type of organizer, because I don't consider them very attractive.

This alcove off a combination living room and family room provides the perfect playroom for children, with tons of customized storage to keep the small space neat as a pin. Segregating play areas like this is a great way to contain and control toy clutter.

sabrina's tip

MAKING SHELVES SPECIAL

There are lots of tricks to make a shelving unit an interesting visual in and of itself. One of the easiest is to paint the inside backing in a shade or tint of your color scheme's primary color. You can also purposefully arrange objects on the shelves in ways that increase graphic appeal. Instead of just a row of books, for example, place some books on their sides for variety and color coordinate them. Blank spaces can be used to good effect as visual pauses that function much as a brief silence does in a piece of music. You can also use an unexpected object such as a shoe mold or a vintage fan to break up a long run of books on a large bookshelf. Rather than just fill the bookshelves as quickly as possible, have a little fun and play around with the placement of whatever's going on those shelves. Don't feel like you have to jam pack your shelves with items. 70 percent capacity is enough.

Bookshelves are often the best places in a room to display decorative accents. The built-in shelves in this living room serve as purely display surfaces.

A large coffee table with compartments serves this informal living room perfectly. Not only does it provide ample hidden storage and large top surface for food, drinks, and magazines, the style matches the relaxed theme of the room, and complements the cushy sectional sofa.

A dedicated shelving unit in a top-floor family room holds everything that the kids of the house might use. The shelves are kept neat and chic with a combination of open shelving, drawers, and wire and fabric bins.

If you or someone in the house is a video gamer, you'll be dealing with video controllers, too. Fortunately, most are wireless these days and can be kept in a box, bin, or other enclosed storage when not in use.

Lastly, control your remotes. Today's home theaters tend to spawn multiple remotes, but you can make sure that they're always close at hand with a dedicated "remote keeper." This can be a large decorative bowl, a mother of pearl box, or one of the many "remote control organizers" you'll find at major retailers. The point is to create one container for all remotes. Once you get used to using it, you'll automatically return remotes to where they're supposed to be.

- Optimize furniture choices. Living rooms and family rooms usually house more pieces of furniture than other rooms. Many of those are "points of opportunity" to create additional hidden storage. A trunk used as a unique coffee table also offers abundant storage. A coffee table with an operable lid and storage space inside is another excellent storage solution. Rather than a simple, standard ottoman, choose one of the many styles of hollow cubes that can double not only as

an ottoman but also as small end tables or coffee tables. (For more ideas, see *The Fifth Layer: Edit Your Furniture.*)

- Control the paper. Ever notice how magazines, newspapers, and other paperwork seem to get ahead of you? It's like they take on a life of their own and multiply at will. A magazine rack is a simple solution that can

The best storage is as stylish as it is useful. This wall-mounted bracket-and-track system exemplifies storage as decorative element, and it brings a whole lot of style to this living room.

Keeping kitchen counters clear is a good way to ensure lots of usable workspace, and to allow the beauty of the countertop to shine through.

also serve as a chic decorative accent. Magazine racks have come a long way since those ugly wire things your aunt and uncle kept in the guest bathroom. There are truly hip bentwood versions; sexy, curved, brushed-aluminum types; and Craftsman-style folding

sabrina's tip

PICTURE THIS!

Young children can't necessarily read labels on boxes, or other storage features. Help your child organize (and prevent frustration for both of you) by "labeling" boxes, bins, and even drawers and shelves, with pictures of what is supposed to go there. You can make it a fun exercise in drawing the items with your youngster, or just take a few pictures with your digital camera and print them out.

units, to mention just a few. I also like to place a decorative bin with a lid in the foyer area so junk mail never makes it into the house.

- **Corral those toys.** Family rooms are all about family. A lot of times, that means children, and children mean toys. My favorite storage solution for keeping toys out of sight when playtime is over are shelving units with slide-out baskets. I find them easier to use than drawers (especially for young children), and they bring a lovely look to the room. I've used wrought-iron frames with wicker basket inserts and plain wood shelves with labeled sheet-metal bins or trays. If those aren't to your taste, you can hide toys in their own trunk or chest, or in the bottom drawers of a larger media center. Whichever way you go, I like to keep toys down low so that they're easy for children to get to—and put back!

the tidy kitchen

A kitchen doesn't need to be messy for it to be disorganized. If you find it a pain to work in the kitchen, poor storage and general disorder are usually to blame. The key is to store kitchen gear as close as possible to where it will be used. Kitchens are also best served—design- and organization-wise—by a well-thought-out combination of hidden and exposed storage. Don't get me wrong; cabinets are probably going to supply most of the general storage space. Cabinet storage is not, however, all that flexible and accommodating. The number and placement of cabinets is constrained by doors, windows, appliances, and countertops. (You'll find a more in-depth discussion about cabinets in *The Fifth Layer: Edit Your Furniture*.)

Think about what you can bring out of your cabinets. One of the things I love about organizing a kitchen is that so many of the tools used to prepare and cook food are visually interesting and can be stored on shelves.

I love to use shelves as complements to cabinetry in a kitchen. It's a natural: lots of easy-to-access space and the chance to display beautiful plates and stemware. If there's no place to comfortably hang a rack, use a wall-mounted floating version. These come with a handy shelf on top to store pots or baking dishes and a bar underneath to hang pans.

No more than four appliances in plain view—preferably fewer.

Exposed storage only works, however, if what you store is out of the way. I'm reluctant to use pot hangers or wall-mounted sliding rails because they often they just look like clutter. Ultimately, kitchens are work areas, and counters and traffic lanes need to be left as clear as possible. I also have a four-appliance rule: no more than four appliances in plain view—preferably fewer.

Slideout racks like these can go a long way toward organizing kitchen cabinet space, and keeping clutter off of countertops.

Kitchen cabinet features and alternatives should be chosen to suit the situation. Here, pull-out drawers under a cooktop make for handy access to pots and pans, while vertical slots prove the best way to organize flat cookware such as cookie sheets and serving trays.

sabrina's tip

PANTRY STYLE

Always paint the inside of your pantry a semi-gloss sheen, and don't be afraid to paint it a bold color, wallpaper, or add tin tiles inside. Also, you can have custom decals made online for all of your plastic containers.

Organizing cabinet interiors will make the room a more pleasant place in which to work. Make the most of corner cabinets by adding rotating shelves; a tiered lazy Susan unit can turn an awkward area into a storage asset. Pull-out shelves are terrific additions to bottom cabinets. I usually spend a little bit more for "drawer" shelves with borders on all sides to hold all those loose plastic containers that collect in any kitchen. I'm also taken with tilt-out plastic under-sink tubs for recyclables and garbage. These tubs help keep your kitchen waste under control. I make good use of all the cabinet organizers available, especially for more specialized storage needs.

SPICE RACKS

You don't have to hide your spices! Not only do they inevitably become a jar jumble when just placed on a shelf, they are also colorful and interesting enough to add to any decor. Instead, organize and proudly display your spice collection by choosing from among the surplus of super spice racks.

- **Traditional spice shelves.** These wall-mounted wood or wrought-iron shelves suit a country or cottage kitchen. They are low-key designs, equipped with rails that hold spices in their original jars (or, less often, in small glass jars supplied by the manufacturer).

- **Test-tube racks.** There's a lot to like about this modern-style spice storage. Spices are kept in glass test-tube containers, topped with corks and stored in wire racks. The tubes show off the spices, and I find them perfect for tapping out just the amount you need. Suppliers offer different numbers of tubes to accommodate more or fewer spices, and the wire racks can be kept on the counter or attached to a wall through tiny screw flanges on the edges. Some suppliers even provide labels so you never mistake the cayenne pepper for the cinnamon (I've been there . . .). The look complements most kitchen styles.

- **Free-standing racks.** Countertop spice racks come in many different styles, although most are mounted on a rotating base to allow easy access. This is a very efficient way for foodies to store a bunch of spices right next to the cooktop—and the designs run from traditional to super mod.

- **Magnetic spice jars.** This type of spice storage has taken off for good reason—it is pure fun. The spices are kept in squat metal jars with magnetic bottoms and see-through tops. The jars are usually arranged on a flat, wall-mounted plate, although I've seen them on the side of a refrigerator or other metal surface. You could even use them in the bathroom. (They won't stick to stainless-steel surfaces, however.)

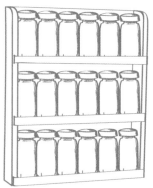

Traditional spice shelf

Test-tube rack

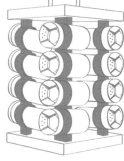

Free-standing rack

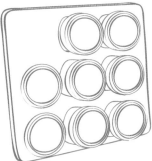

Magnetic spice jars

Whenever I'm helping a client get a kitchen or pantry in order, I buy plastic or glass containers (you want to able to see what's inside).

Cabinets aside, you may be one of those lucky individuals who has a pantry closet. A pantry of any size needs to be well organized if it's going to be as useful as it should be. First off, store like with like, and try to group by type of food and size of container. Whenever I'm helping a client get a kitchen or pantry in order, I buy plastic or glass containers (you want to able to see what's inside) of various sizes to hold loose, bagged food such as rice, oatmeal, or bulk cereals. Adding slide-out trays and shelf organizers makes an easy task of rotating stock. You can also use over-door organizers with pockets and shelves of various sizes to add significant storage to the back of a pantry door.

The dining room is, for me, an extension of the kitchen where storage is concerned. I've always believed that less is definitely more in the dining room, from both a design and a use perspective. There is a tendency to buy large pieces of furniture to store what is rarely used, such as china, crystal, and special-occasion linens. But in reality, dining room table settings can usually find a suitable home in the back of an upper kitchen cabinet or in those hard-to-reach high cabinets over the refrigerator. Other heritage pieces such as special serving plates or silver coffee urns can also be stored in the kitchen or, if you have one, in the dining room closet. Linens such as napkins and tablecloths can be placed in a hall closet, or where your towels and other linens are stored.

This sun-washed dining room is well served by a single sideboard with a broad top surface for dishes from the kitchen, and a lot of drawer space. Stemware, servers, utensils, and dishware are all stored in the kitchen.

sabrina's tip

BOWLED OVER

Free up cabinet space and decorate your countertops at the same time with a trio (or duo, quartet, whatever) of pretty bowls. They can hold fruit, breakfast bars, fresh produce such as avocados and tomatoes, and other loose items. It's a great way to add splashes of color and keep foodstuffs out where you can see and use them before they spoil.

a shipshape bathroom

Bathroom floors are magnets. They magically attract clothes, washcloths, towels, and just about any other piece of fabric that makes its way into the room. For some reason, when you're rushed

sabrina's tip

CURTAIN CAMEO

A homeowner on one of my shows had a small, cluttered bathroom that desperately needed order and organization. The chief eyesore in the room was a three-drawer plastic rolling unit. It not only looked cheap, but it was stuffed with a jumble of cosmetics and personal care products. I had the homeowner weed out her collection (makeup has an expiration date!), and we organized what was left in the pockets of a brand-new plastic shower curtain, facing out and hidden behind a beautiful shower curtain. The pockets kept everything she needed within easy reach, and they were on the outside of the curtain, so water wasn't an issue.

or tired, it just seems like too much effort to walk a pile of clothes out to a hamper. I get it. I'm like that, too. It's all the more reason to add a hamper as part of a bathroom design project. Hang a laundry bag on a hook, on the back of the door, in an informal bathroom. More likely, though, you'll want a somewhat more polished look. Ten minutes spent scanning a couple of catalogs will turn up lacquered hampers, rattan and wicker, wood with woven venting screens, cotton duck hamper bags made portable in a rolling frame, glass-beaded hamper bins with lids, and many more options. Incorporate a wall-mounted tip-out hamper cabinet, or retrofit the under-sink space in a large vanity.

Providing adequate space for towels is also crucial to keeping the bathroom squared away. Don't just put up a single hanging bar and think

When a bathroom has a closet, take the time to organize it for what needs to be stored, rather than just storing things in available space. The pantry-style closet in this bathroom accommodates everything that could possibly be needed in the space, and the bi-fold doors are perfect for the small room.

it will do the job because it holds two towels. Damp towels need a place to dry out. I like to use towel racks that hang on the back of the door for everyday use. Add a touch of luxury to your bathroom with a wall-mounted, heated towel rack, but use one that is hard-wired into an electrical circuit. I prefer the plainer chrome styles because the simple elegance suits any decor.

A little extra hidden storage always comes in handy in a bathroom. (Nobody wants to run out of toilet paper at a crucial moment.) When adding this type of storage, I look for the most convenient location. Wall-mounted accessory cabinets can be placed right over the toilet, and they come in just about every style imaginable. However, you may prefer free-standing storage. You can repurpose general cabinets in the bathroom, but I find that it's a lot easier to shop the huge selection of free-standing cabinets designed specifically for the tighter spaces in a bathroom. Tall and skinny units easily tuck between a toilet and a vanity or nestle into a corner. Pick one with adjustable shelves, because flexibility is essential.

> Clutter isn't just annoying; it's a design killer.

Vanity-top clutter is a major source of disorder in a bathroom. Skincare and hair-care products, makeup and makeup brushes, and much, much more overflow the limited capacity of most medicine cabinets. The best way to keep these small items under control is by "containerizing."

The last bathroom area to organize is the inside of the shower or bath. Homeowners often put up with disorder here because visitors rarely see behind the shower curtain or sliding doors. It's important to organize the space to make it more efficient and easier to clean. I lean toward adjustable pole organizers that fit into the corner and include several shelves. There are other

types, including those that hang from the neck of the showerhead or the curtain rod, and more permanent options that can be screwed right into the tile. Regardless of which you choose, make sure it is capable of holding everything you use in the shower or bath . . . and is rust-proof!

a bedroom sanctuary

The bedroom should be a place so comfortable that great sleep is a guarantee. A disorganized bedroom creates the opposite feeling, one of tension and discord. Fortunately, organizing this room is a matter of some simple and logical strategies. The best prevent future disorganization and keep the room looking its best at all times.

Start with the furniture. Bedroom furnishings should do double duty whenever possible. Beds can be storage as well as centerpieces. A platform bed with drawers in the platform, or a bed on a hydraulic system, can supply a lot of storage, often circumventing the need for a dresser. The look isn't for everyone; you may decide that you want to stick with your simple metal frame, box spring, and mattress. The under-bed area of a more traditional bed is

sabrina's rule

DON'T BE TRAPPED WITH YOUR SET

Bedroom furniture is often sold in sets or suites, but that doesn't mean you have to use every piece you buy. All too often, I see homeowners cramming every piece of a bedroom set into a much-too-small bedroom. It's not uncommon that I find the drawers half-filled or empty, while the homeowners need someplace to store seasonal bedding, extra pillows, and other large items. If you are including a piece of storage furniture in the bedroom—or any room, for that matter—just because it's part of a set, you are not making good use of the space. Don't be afraid to break up or mix and match a set and sell or donate the pieces you don't really need or can't use.

Use only the storage furniture you need. Although two bed tables is the most common layout, a single piece better serves a one-person bedroom and leaves more open floor space.

prime real estate for hidden storage. Slide-under drawer units are available in metal, wood, and plastic. Some are designed to show along the bottom edges of the bed, while most are meant to be slid entirely under and out of view. Inexpensive clear or fogged plastic units let you see what's stored at a glance.

Your choice of bedside tables can also pick up storage slack. Side tables with drawers are great for hiding away all those bits and pieces that can make

a mess of surfaces alongside the bed (eyeglasses, remote for the bedroom TV, books and magazines, nighttime medications, and so on). Nightstands with shelves also work nicely. A decorative basket could hold throw pillows and blankets.

As much as a bed frame or nightstands can help out, the key storage piece of furniture in the bedroom is usually the dresser. Make your dresser much more efficient and useful by adding drawer organizers or dividers. Simple divider walls added to a sock drawer can turn a messy mishmash of sock singles into neat rows of rolled-up pairs. A drawer organizer or jewelry caddy can impose order on any drawer. Because organization is so closely related to use in the bedroom, streamlining and improving something as simple as dresser drawers can save you tons of time and frustration when you're getting dressed.

correctly configured closets

Closets are the heart of any bedroom's organization. They are also the room's biggest challenge. I rarely, if ever, leave the closets as they are when I design a

sabrina's tip

CHIC CLOSET SYSTEMS

We live in wonderful times. You don't need to assemble your perfect closet design element by element, because major retailers do it for you. Several stores supply turnkey solutions that can be customized to your closet's size and your storage needs. These are available in three basic levels of quality and expense.

The least expensive are steel wire systems with racks, wire drawers, or bins that clip onto the racks, and a limited number of additional accessories. The racks are cut to fit with wire snips or special cutters, and manufacturers provide rubber tips for exposed ends. These are groovy for kid's closets, but I don't usually use them in adult bedrooms because the racks leave lines on more delicate clothes and the look generally isn't on par with an adult bedroom design.

The next level up are systems with more durable components, including solid melamine or MDF (medium-density fiberboard) shelves and dividers, drawer units of the same material, and accessories such as shoe cubbies. Like high-end units, these are usually offered as complete custom systems. Either the store will assign you a designer, or you give the supplier the closet's dimensions and the features you want, and they design and deliver the components to fit.

At the top end are luxury closet systems with pure wood or wood veneer shelves and dividers, sleek drawer designs mounted on roller-bearing tracks, and a multitude of special features such as powered tie racks, adjustable shelving, and slanted shoe racks.

This dark wood closet system exhibits the range of available storage options, including cabinets (with decorative frosted inserts in this case), drawer, standard and special canted (angled) shelves, and abundant hanging storage.

bedroom. The key to savvy closets is configuration. By that I mean how and where you locate hanging storage, what shelving you use, and what other features you add.

It's smart to begin with the hanging storage, because that's where people make the most mistakes. As a rule, a man's closet (or the man's side of the closet) is rarely well served with a single hanging bar. Men's clothing can all be hung half-height, which means that you can stack two hanging bars, pretty much doubling the hanging storage. The vertical space necessary to accommodate suits, shirts, and pants folded over a hanger is 45 inches. Women tend to own longer garments such as dresses that must be hung full-length, requiring at least 72 inches of vertical space. When configuring your closet, always allow more room than you think you'll need; clothes last longer and look nicer when they are not crammed into place.

Let's be clear here: Everything you're currently hanging up may not need to be hung. Casual

pants (men's and women's) such as jeans or khakis should be folded and stored on a shelf or in a drawer. If you use your dress shirts straight from the dry cleaner, have them box the shirts so you can store them on a shelf. Scarves, ties, belts, and other accessories should never take up space on a hanger. More about those in a second.

Shelves are perfect complements to hanging closet storage and can be the ideal place for stacked sweaters, blankets, and other foldable items. You can increase the usefulness of shelves by using labeled boxes to hold smaller loose items such as gloves or caps and seasonal or specialty garments such as ski clothes. Shallower, labeled bins can stand in for dresser drawers as places for bras and panties.

Footwear calls for its own storage. If the number of shoes is minimal, a simple organizer will do the trick. Just make sure you buy one with enough room for all your shoes. However, if you own a lot of shoes, give some serious thought to dedicated

shoe shelves or *cubbies*. These can be flat shelves, 12 inches deep and 4 inches high (toes in so that the shoes are easy to grab on the fly), or canted shelves with a ledge to hold the shoes in place. Either way, allow 8 to 10 inches of space for each pair of shoes. Cubbies are my second choice because the number of shoes you own changes over time and the number of cubbies won't. They also don't work well for boots.

Properly organized accessories are the icing on the cake that is your closet. This can mean adding a column of drawers or using specialty hanging or shelf organizers. I like to hang belts from hooks, although they can also be rolled up and stored in drawers separated by dividers. (In my experience, though, most people aren't going to hassle with rolling up their belts or ties.) Ties can be hung

Top: A slide-out panel like this one can add significantly to the storage in either a walk-in or a reach-in closet.

Bottom: A tie rack keeps a man's neckwear organized and in good condition. The pull-out type shown here couldn't be handier.

Drawer inserts are small additions that can make a big difference in keeping small valuables in order and right where you need them. This type of insert can be used in a closet drawer, dresser, or even a nightstand, depending on what you need to store.

sabrina's tip

REPLICATING RETAIL FLAIR

Retail clothing stores have the inside scoop on how to store clothing out in the open in a visually stunning display. Professionals create inviting shelf or table displays of folded sweaters, pants, and other garments. If you can't afford a stylist of your own, you can cadge a few tricks of the trade just by carefully observing these displays and copying what they do. Sweaters and shirts are stacked with the fold facing the viewer—creating a nicer appearance and making it easier to pull out a single sweater without totally disrupting the pile. Display designers also tend to group garments by color and/or shade to create a simplified visual that appeals to the eye. These pros also follow a basic logic that you should use in your closets and on your shelves: smaller items on top of larger ones, clothing piled no more than 12 inches high, and a small amount of space left between adjacent piles.

from wall- or bar-mounted tie racks. The same is true of scarves—if they need to be hung. Simple hooks on the back of the closet door or on the back or side walls of the closet can serve nicely as scarf storage. Go a little fancier with specialty drawer inserts custom-made to hold watches, earrings, necklaces, and other jewelry.

I look at shelves in the bedroom as overflow valves for the closet and elsewhere. Wall-mounted shelves are great places for the more attractive textiles in the room.

The right combination of these is sure to organize your bedroom in high style, whether you're designing a master suite or more modest guest quarters. These storage solutions and strategies will even work perfectly for kids' rooms, with a few additions or changes.

adapting (and adaptable) storage for kids' rooms

Kids' rooms call for storage furniture and solutions that can grow and adapt from age to age. When I design a kid's bedroom—regardless of age—I look for natural materials that can be painted and repainted as "what's cool" changes. I stay away from cartoon characters, quick-to-age storage furniture such as plastic toy chests that look like treasure chests, and specialty beds.

The storage in your son's or daughter's closet has to be even more obvious and intuitive than it is in other bedrooms. I always give kids their own laundry hamper to reinforce the idea that floors, beds, and desk chairs are not suitable resting places for dirty shirts or jeans. In all cases except for pre-teen and teen girls, you need only a minimal amount of hanging storage (if any) in a kid's closet. Most of what they wear can be folded and put on a shelf or a drawer, so those structures should take up the most room in the closet. (I use wire racks, dividers, and bins for a kid's closet because you'll probably be changing the configuration in short order.) Hooks are also excellent additions to a kid's closet; I use

This neat and attractive display of sweaters and shoes could have come right out of a store.

The closet in this pre-teen girl's bedroom is perfectly set up for the room's occupant. Minimal hanging storage and lots of bins and shelves ensure there is a place for everything to go. Replacing closet doors with a curtain on a decorative rod is a nice touch that allowed even more personalization in the choice of fabric.

decorative hook-and-shelf combinations on walls (positioned at the appropriate height for the room's occupant) to supplement closet storage.

I also have a little fun with labeling like using pictures instead of words, especially for younger kids. You can create funky labels for drawers, boxes, bins, or baskets. It's a way to head off those annoying "Mom, where's my . . . ?" questions and increase the likelihood that fresh laundry will be put where it belongs.

a well-contained home office

The truth about home offices is that they are rarely given a room to themselves. More often than not, even when someone works from home full-time, the home office is carved out of other existing space. It can be half a guest bedroom or a quiet corner of a large family room—I've even used a closet converted into a nifty little office! Even if you're lucky enough to have an entire extra room of dedicated professional space, the strategies that follow will work just the same.

The best home office storage is all about blending and hiding. There is simply no reason to sacrifice great looks for productivity. When just about everything you use for work has a place to go, your desk will look organized and tidy and you'll work more efficiently.

Paperwork is the number-one culprit in an untidy office, and paper clutter has a way of migrating to other rooms. That's why I always push my clients to go digital. I'm not a techie, but honestly, an easy-to-use, good-quality scanner is inexpensive and really useful. So there's really no reason not to digitize your home office documents and paperwork. I also like using Bluetooth and wireless office equipment to eliminate as many cables as possible.

Your work desk is going to be command central of your home office. I'm especially fond of work desks with specialized drawers for holding and hiding away printers, scanners, and other office equipment.

A room dedicated to a home office calls for multi-faceted storage like this shelf unit. It offers abundant hidden and easily accessible exposed storage, all wrapped in a beautiful wood package.

Alcoves can be perfect locations for a compact home office, especially when you equip it with the kind of storage featured in this bright spot. Shelves, cabinets, and a desk surface between two walls create a perfect place to get work done.

File cabinets also come into play, and not just for filing. Many units include drawers or shelves above the hanging file drawer. I like this because it makes the storage unit more adaptable. You'll also find units that look just like file cabinets but with drawers designed to hold printers, small copiers, or scanners. I love the idea of pulling out a drawer when you need to print something, but otherwise never seeing your printer.

Actual file cabinets are available in vertical or horizontal configurations, as rolling units, and as simple desktop brackets. As I've said, it's best to find one that holds all your paperwork in neat order and blends seamlessly into the decor.

I complement desk and file cabinet storage with color- or texture-coordinated boxes or bins of various sizes. You'll find coordinated sets at office supply stores, including boxes big enough for file folders and small enough to hold pens or paper clips. You can also kick your imagination into high gear and repurpose a set of boxes, tins, or other containers from nonwork parts of your life. Regardless of where the containers come from, containerize everything you can, and if needed, label each container.

Those containers are most likely going to find a home on a shelf. I make it a rule to locate a home office desk near a large shelving unit, or vice versa. I particularly like units with adjustable shelves so that you can play with spacing to fit various office materials and changing professional demands and resources. Position the desk, shelving, and any other storage and equipment in fairly tight proximity so that everything can be reached within a few feet of where you do your work.

Cable organizers are a must for the organized office! These days, many desks have them built right in, with hidden channels and cable holes like this desk grommet to guide them where you want cables to go.

Perhaps the single biggest visual blemish a home office makes on a room design is cable clutter. There's just no excuse for it. There are many different ways to contain and control cables and wires. All of them are simple to install and use. You'll find plastic snap-in channels that neatly organize groups of cables and that have adhesive backs or screw flanges that allow them to be attached to the underside or back side of desk. Large bunches of cables can be contained in a flexible cord conduit. The conduit can be run just about anywhere and keeps cables safe from damage. You can use the same solutions for the cables that serve your entertainment center in a family room, or anywhere else in the house that electronics congregate.

Spend some time planning how you'll organize the space you're designing, and you'll ensure that not only will it look good all the time, but it will be that much easier to do whatever it is you do there. When you're absolutely sure that you've got your storage options and clutter-killing strategies lined up, you're ready to tackle the task of editing your furniture.

the fifth layer
edit your furniture

It's the rare homeowner who has the option to put together an entirely new and completely coordinated collection of furniture from scratch. The truth is, we usually collect furniture along life's path. Some are accidental acquisitions, things you find on sale at a local furniture store, or really cool pieces you stumble across at a flea market. Others come to us with special meanings, like that designer sofa you saved for years to buy, or your grandmother's Duncan Phyfe dining room table and chairs. Even these special pieces, though, are added to a pretty diverse group.

That reality is why I use the word *edit* rather than *buy* in the title of this layer. Heck, I'd love to run right out and buy all new furniture every time I redecorate a home, but that's not realistic. Yes, occasionally you'll need to buy a new piece to replace an old one that is just too far gone to save, or because of new circumstances or spaces. More often, though, you can create a fantastic room setting by repositioning or reviving your existing furniture. The change can be as basic as moving a sofa to a more logical position, or it can involve a bigger undertaking, like stripping and repainting a bedroom dresser. Whatever the case, I'm a big one for repurposing furniture. There's so much you can do to save even timeworn pieces, and why not save money wherever you can?

However, before you start sanding down tabletops or refinishing chairs, you have to decide what must go, what should stay, and where to put everything. The ultimate goal is a compelling room layout that creates a beautiful room that is easy to navigate and use.

spotlight on centerpieces

The first step down the road that leads to a fabulously furnished room is establishing the *centerpieces*. Centerpieces are the main furnishings that define what a room is all about. The bed and nightstands in the bedroom are centerpieces, as is the combo of seating, console table, and mirror in an entryway. Living room centerpieces usually include the couch, easy chairs and coffee table. Family room centerpieces can be a little tougher to pin down, but they're generally the casual seating placed facing the entertainment center.

No matter what room they're in, all centerpieces set the tone for the other furnishings and decorative elements. That's why you position them first. Their placement anchors the layout, determining where other furnishings and features will go (not to mention how user-friendly the room will be). That's why it really pays to get the centerpiece location right. First and foremost, they shouldn't clash with any of the design goals that you identified in *The First Layer: Understand Your Space and Plan Your Design*. I look for centerpieces to complement the lines and features of the room (or specifically contrast them, if that's what you're after).

Before finalizing your centerpieces, cast a critical eye over the furniture you originally moved out of the room. In many cases, you'll be able to revive furniture to suit the new design. I generally only replace a piece of furniture when the actual structure has been compromised, or when the piece is entirely out of scale.

By out of scale, I mean that a piece of furniture is too large, too small, or entirely the wrong shape

Previous page: The basic living room centerpiece grouping of sofa, easy chairs, and coffee table is incredibly adaptable and can serve any style of living room.

Notice how a well-placed area rug helps tie the grouping together visually.

for the size of the room and the other furnishings. Not only will an odd-sized piece look strange with other furnishings, it's also likely to mess up the layout. There's an easy way to determine if any given piece fits comfortably in the room's layout, which is the cue to put that room sketch that you made in the first layer to good use.

Perfect your layout—and your style—by putting the right furnishings in the right places.

Grab some poster board or thick paper, and cut out shapes to represent your furniture (remember to use the same scale that you used for the original sketch!). Now you can easily play with positioning by moving the cutouts around on the sketch. That's a lot easier than moving real furniture around. This should give you a good sense of how the centerpieces relate to the space, and it's a great way to quickly find the best positioning. It will also tell you in no uncertain terms if a given piece simply won't work in the room.

Centerpieces don't have to be flashy to be effective. This small, spare, and elegant table and chairs set the tone for a room that is restrained and perfectly lovely.

With a large coffee table centered on a rug of the same shape, this furniture grouping anchors the whole room and provides a base upon which the room's design can be built.

Any layout needs to accommodate the space's special features. This sectional sofa is left isolated in a large, open space to allow a concealed bed to drop down from the wall when an extra bedroom is needed.

sabrina's rule

KEEP CORRECT SPACING

The right room layout allows adequate space for easy movement around furniture. Use the measurements below as minimums.

- Allow for 3-foot-wide traffic lanes through a room.
- Allow 36 inches in all directions from the door of a room to any piece of furniture.
- Allow 18–20 inches between the edge of the couch and the coffee table. (Save those knees, people!)
- Maintain between 4 and 9 feet of distance between a sofa and chairs in a conversation area. Too far away is as bad as too close.
- Maintain three times the diagonal measurement of the TV between the screen and the seated viewer (that is, you should leave 9 feet between the TV and couch seat for a 36-inch screen).
- Allow 24 inches between the bottom edge of a bed (not necessarily the mattress—whichever part sticks out the farthest) and a wall or other furniture. This ensures that bed linens can easily be stripped and the bed easily made.
- Maintain 36 inches between the edge of a dining room table and the wall, to allow for seated diners. Add an additional 12 inches if you want to allow free passage behind seated guests. Each place setting should allow 24 inches of table space side to side and at least 16 inches from the edge toward the center of the table.

The focal point of this bedroom is obvious from the floorboard direction and the symmetrical placement of twin easy chairs that frame a sleeping alcove. The plush bed invites anyone in the room to recline and relax.

As you position the centerpieces, make the room easy to navigate. Here are a few guidelines for doing just that:

- Avoid creating "dead zones" by blocking off sections of a room.

- Keep an eye on the natural light in the room and place furniture accordingly. For instance, if you're adding a home office in the corner of a living room, don't place your computer monitor across from a window that receives strong light, or you'll fight glare all day long.

- Frame the intended focal point(s) in the room. For instance, in a living room where you want to showcase a stunning fireplace, the centerpiece furnishings—sofa, chairs, and coffee table—should be placed so that all the seating faces or partially faces the fireplace. If the room has a large window with a stunning view, it's not wise to position seating with its back to the large window.

Sometimes, centerpiece location is obvious, especially where there's only one real option. For instance, in a small bedroom or a child's room, there is often only one logical place and one orientation for the bed and nightstands. Getting it right in other rooms, such as a large, L-shaped living room, may require a bit more trial and error.

Where furniture positioning isn't fairly obvious, turn to the notes you made in the first layer. You should start with practical aspects. Will the sun be in your eyes if you're sitting in a chair or on a couch? Do you want the centerpieces under the room's only overhead light? Are you looking to focus on an architectural feature such as a fireplace? How will you use the furniture? Answer the practical questions like these and you'll find your way to the ideal centerpiece location and, from there, to the most effective layout.

Stools can be great options for an island dining area. These stools slide right under the edge of the counter, keeping the traffic lane behind them open—an important visual element in an open floor plan such as this.

You couldn't ask for a better focal point than a gas fireplace topped with a flat-panel TV, all captured in a smooth quartz structure set in front of a stacked flagstone column. Positioning the TV over the fireplace is a natural marriage that has become extremely popular because of today's flat, wall-mounted units.

refine your rooms

Once you've got your centerpieces in place, fill in the layout by placing secondary pieces. Many homes are a little overfurnished because homeowners understandably collect furniture over time, and it can be difficult to keep in mind what role any particular piece will play. People move to new houses and take along their old furniture. It's easy to fall into the trap of thinking that because you own a piece of furniture, you have to use it. The reality is that the sideboard you bought for your first house may be entirely wrong for your new home's dining room. Be fearless. Really editing furniture means adapting furniture to the design as much as possible. Unfortunately, sometimes it also means getting rid of pieces that just don't work.

sabrina's rule
DON'T DUMP!

As you edit your furniture, you'll probably find that some pieces don't make the cut. That's okay, but don't just set them on the curb or haul them to the junkyard where they'll take up valuable space in overcrowded landfills. Instead, donate them to Goodwill or give them away to family or friends, post a notice on the bulletin boards at local retailers, or offer them on a site like Craigslist.org (which has a "free" section).

Placing secondary pieces starts with positioning the storage features you identified in *The Fourth Layer: Integrate Storage to Organize Your Space*.

Where space allows, secondary furnishings can help define a room. This wide-open, dark, and dramatic bedroom includes an entire sitting area that creates a multi-faceted layout.

Set free-standing and wall-mounted shelving units in place, and position other pieces meant specifically for storage such as chests for toys. These are all functional parts of the design, which is why they need to be in place before you add any other secondary furnishings. As I discussed in the fourth layer, storage features should never look tacked on, and they should not impede the room's layout.

Keep building your layout using the scale cutouts on your original sketch. When you think you've

found the perfect home for a secondary piece, tape it down. As you work along, ask yourself the all-important questions:

- What else needs to be here?
- What other types of seating do I need?
- Am I leaving appropriate space for traffic in and through the room?
- What pieces will round out the look of the room *and* make it more usable?
- What furniture would really complement the centerpieces?
- What furniture is overkill, too large, or out of place?

Those can be difficult questions. Believe me, I know. Thinking through the answers will lead you to secondary furnishings that really add something to your interior design rather than just take up space. Of course, you still have to judge each individual piece on the criteria we use for almost every part of the design: lines that suit the space and other furniture, colors that work with the color

sabrina's tip

LITERARY FURNISHINGS

Put your books to work as furniture. Stack large-format coffee-table books to use as an intriguing end table or nightstand. You'll not only free up the storage space the books would have required, but you'll also need one less end table.

scheme, forms and textures that complement your design. A lot of times I'm able to seamlessly integrate what would otherwise be an eyesore piece of furniture into a room design and layout simply by painting or staining it to match the general color scheme. It's easy to repurpose a couch that has good bones but the wrong color or fabric; all it takes is reupholstering in a nicer fabric.

Throughout this part of the process, keep visual balance in mind. A giant, bulky country wardrobe might seem ideal for holding all your home entertainment gear, but not if it overshadows the modern, low-slung couch and simple square coffee table you've already chosen as your centerpieces. A delicate dresser won't work in your bedroom if all the other furnishings are bulky, contemporary pieces with rounded edges and supersized proportions.

editing furniture throughout the house

I hope that by now you're seeing the method to my madness: Develop the heart of the room's layout by choosing and placing the primary centerpieces. Then position your storage features, ensuring they don't disrupt the natural flow of the room. Finally, put the remaining secondary furnishings in place. Simple, right?

sabrina's rule
BUY QUALITY

Furniture is an investment. Cheap furniture tends to wear out unreasonably and ages much quicker than high-quality pieces would. Judge furniture on its quality of construction, and you'll likely wind up with a piece that may save you money in the long run.

- **Solid wood.** True of both furniture frames and visible surface, solid wood is stronger, more durable, and longer lasting than other materials.
- **Corner blocks.** Corner blocks are quality indicators in tables of all kinds, nightstands, seating, and cabinetry. They help furnishings maintain their shape and should be screwed and glued in place, not just glued.
- **Dovetailed or mortise-and-tenon.** How pieces are joined at their edges is a true sign of craftsmanship. The best furniture joints are dovetailed or mortise-in-tenon—both are visible as interlocking joints as shown in the photo. Joints that are simply butted together (called butt joints) are a less durable form of construction.
- **Dust panels.** Thin partitions between adjacent drawers in *case* furniture (pieces such as hutches meant strictly for storage) and desks are evidence of detailed construction.
- **Back panels.** The best shelving and other standing furniture features back panels that are invisible from the side. They are usually slid into recessed channels in the sides of the piece or nailed in an edge channel. This construction adds to the overall strength of the furniture.

This eclectic living room is centered around a seating group with borders defined by a flokati wool rug. Notice the space left all around the grouping; traffic moving through the room does not need to impede on this well-defined area.

Now we'll bring it down to earth by looking at actual rooms. Take a walk with me through an imaginary model house as we furnish real rooms. You know how much I love rules (even if I break them from time to time), so along the way I'll give you basic guidelines to help you select and place furniture in each room.

the basic entry suite

My rules for entryway furniture are: Make the transition easy, give hints about what to expect in the rest of the house, and shout "welcome!" I don't normally include much more than the centerpieces of console table, seating, and a mirror.

Err on the side of modesty in picking an entryway table. I've occasionally incorporated stylish dressers or sideboards in large entry halls that see a lot of traffic and can make good use of the extra storage. Those were special cases, though, where I lucked onto just the right piece for the size, shape, and design of the space. If you have a hankering to use an unusual piece of furniture as a hall table, make sure that it doesn't block the layout.

Seating is another entryway essential, and the one most often neglected. Part of making an entryway welcoming is giving people a place to sit down and take off their shoes. It's also nice to have a comfortable place to wait while your better half gets ready. I've seen a lot of eye-catching chair used, but I'm partial to something a little more substantial, like a bench. People wrestling themselves out of heavy cold-weather garments or boots tend to need more space than a chair provides, and a chair may not be up to the wear and tear. The thing I really love about benches is that it's so easy to find one to match your decor. A unit with a baskets along the bottom brace is great for a house with kids or a lot of visitors. I've repainted an outdoor bench and added lovely cushions to create a one-of-a-kind entryway perch. The point is, don't hesitate to look in unlikely places for just the right entryway seating.

A mirror is crucial in the entryway, not only for your last look on the way out the door, but also to add personality to what is often a relatively small, bland space. I use a mirror that is as large as possible while still looking appropriate on the available wall space.

As basic and functional as entryways are, I rarely include secondary pieces. If the closet is a little tight (or there isn't one) and floor space isn't an issue, you've probably already planned for a stand-alone coat rack and/or umbrella stand (the perfect opportunity to personalize the space with a flash of color, an unusual material such as hammered metal, or an interesting form).

sabrina's tip

A LOVELY LOOKING GLASS

Don't you dare pay full price for a mirror! With a little legwork, you can find a unique and interesting mirror at a bargain price. They are one of the most common items for sale at flea markets, estate sales, yard and garage sales, and thrift shops. Even if you don't like the frame, or the mirror doesn't have one, framing a mirror is an easy project. You can even hang an unframed mirror with hidden hangers for a clean, sleek look.

A gold-frame mirror adds a touch of elegance to a dramatic foyer. The curvy mirror plays off the shape of the sweeping staircase and adds both form and function to the space.

Left: This well-appointed entryway features the essential furniture necessary to make the space useful, comfortable, and stylish without cluttering the design.

Ideally, entryway furnishings should reveal colors, lines, textures, or forms that will be found in the rest of the house. This doesn't mean the entryway should look like a miniature of your living room; it just needs to feature one or two key indicators, such as a furniture leg style that mimics the console table in the living room or the dining room table legs.

truly livable living rooms

Now let's move into the living room. I've helped many people rescue their living rooms from design chaos, and the number-one problem I encounter is furniture clutter. The space just seems to invite furniture strays. This is understandable because this particular room usually has to fill several different roles—a place to relax, a social center for entertaining and parties, a space for family get-togethers, and more.

That's why my furniture rule for this multifaceted room is: No reason for being means no being in the living room. You should be able to clearly state your rationale for including any given piece of furniture. It can be as simple as "I need a surface for that great table lamp," or it can be more practical, such as "We need extra seating for all the entertaining we do."

My rule for family room furniture is: Focus on comfort and durability while maintaining established design cues.

An informal centerpiece grouping makes for an engaging focal point in a living room. The chunky, linear coffee table perfectly complements the straight lines and squared-off shapes of the seating, tying the whole group together.

This living room is typical of the common contemporary trend of putting a TV over a fireplace. Flat-panel TVs read as graphic shapes when turned off, and work perfectly over a fireplace. Handsome twin shelving units create the perfect entertainment center and add general storage on either side of the fireplace column. I like how the setup creates a visual balance that is counteracted by the eclectic nature of the furniture.

A family room shares some roles with the living room, so it makes sense to talk about family room furnishings here. Not every home has a family room, but even if yours doesn't, the principles that guide choosing and placing family room furniture apply equally to a dedicated entertainment or play area in a big living room. My rule for family room furniture is: Focus on comfort and durability while maintaining established design cues. For instance, I often use more stout and sturdy pieces in a family room, but ones with the same lines, fabric, and colors of furniture used in other rooms.

If the room is large enough, I'll create independent activity areas with secondary furniture. Focus on what you like to do there. Do you entertain a lot? If so, you might want to make one or two conversation areas, with simple, comfortable chairs grouped around a smaller table, mimicking the centerpiece grouping. This is also the perfect way to make a large, open floor plan seem more intimate and inviting. Are you a book junkie? Create your own little literary enclave by combining a comfortable chair, a small side table, and a good reading lamp in an out-of-the-way corner of the room.

sabrina's tip

RECLINE WITH FLAIR

I'm risking some dirty looks here, but I'll say it anyway: I'm not real fond of recliners. As comfortable as they can be, they tend to look like, well, recliners. However, I must admit that today's versions are much more stylish than ever before. If a client prefers a reclining easy chair, I'll steer him toward the high end, where you can find styles that look like leather club chairs or sophisticated Craftsman-style seating. Spend just a little bit more and you'll be able to choose a recliner that looks like anything but a recliner.

THE ALL-PURPOSE CUBE

I really like the stand-alone cubes you see everywhere these days. They are incredibly adaptable secondary pieces for the living room and beyond. Available in different woods and finishes, or upholstered in leather or fabric, there's a style that's just right for your decor. What I really like about cubes—besides the simple shape that complements most interior designs—is that they usually have a storage cavity inside. They can be additional seating around a coffee table, an ottoman for an easy chair, or—used in a group of two or three—a cool stand-in for a coffee table.

CHIC SOFAS

When it comes to living room seating, the one piece that absolutely must be in the mix is a good sofa. Sofa style is usually determined by whether or not the legs are shown, the construction of the arms, the number and placement of cushions, and the shape of the back. Thankfully, there's no lack of lovely styles to choose from.

- **Club.** Sometimes called "English," this style is both comfortable and somewhat prim. The structure includes rounded, fully stuffed cushions; low, rounded arms; and a skirtless base with decorative legs that are usually equipped with casters. A club sofa bridges many decors, and I would use one in any but a modern living room.

- **Bridgewater.** This is the most popular contemporary style. Rolled arms, three full seat and back cushions, and a pleated skirt all add to a look that invites sitting and sprawling. You can confidently include a bridgewater-style sofa in almost any living room.

- **Tuxedo.** You'll find several variations of this classic, but all have a squared-off, streamlined look. The stereotypical tuxedo sofa features high, squared arms and back, all at the same level (the arms are sometimes flared out as shown on the right). The back and sides form tall walls that surround the cushions. With a few additional pillows, this sofa can be really cozy, and the clean, linear appearance blends with many different room styles.

- **Chesterfield.** Similar to the tuxedo in that the back and arms are at the same height, a chesterfield sofa has rounded arms and back, and the sofa is often tufted.

- **Lawson.** The Lawson style is a no-nonsense and handsome look that suits many interior designs. It is squared-off and slightly chunky, with low arms, a straight back, and exposed block feet. Lawson sofas often feature piping that accentuates the linear look. I wouldn't hesitate to incorporate a Lawson sofa into a modern, contemporary, or even traditional interior. The only room in which it would look out of place is one filled with ornamentation, curvy overstuffed furnishings, and billowy window treatments.

- **Modern.** Modern sofas are distinguished by minimal detailing and linear forms that make for a sleek appearance. More often than not, modern styles do not have separate cushions, and they usually include open spaces underneath that show off metal or simply styled legs. These sofas can slip right into a contemporary interior design focused on simple linear forms and minimal decorations. They are most at home, however, in a truly modern room.

- **Camelback.** This sofa gets its name from the signature curving back that looks somewhat like a hump (some versions feature two "humps"). The style dates back more than a century, when it was crafted as a smaller, skirtless sofa. Today's crop of camelback sofas include those with skirts and without, rolled and simple wood arms, and many other variations. Depending on which fabric you choose, a camelback sofa could fit into just about any interior.

- **Sectional.** A modern-era innovation, the sectional sofa offers abundant comfortable seating adaptable to different room layouts. Sectionals come in all kinds of designs, from overstuffed leather versions to sleek modern types. I find that the most useful are those that allow the "leg" of the sofa to be positioned on either side of the main body of the unit. Because of the size and expense, I use sectional sofas only in large rooms where the additional seating is clearly needed.

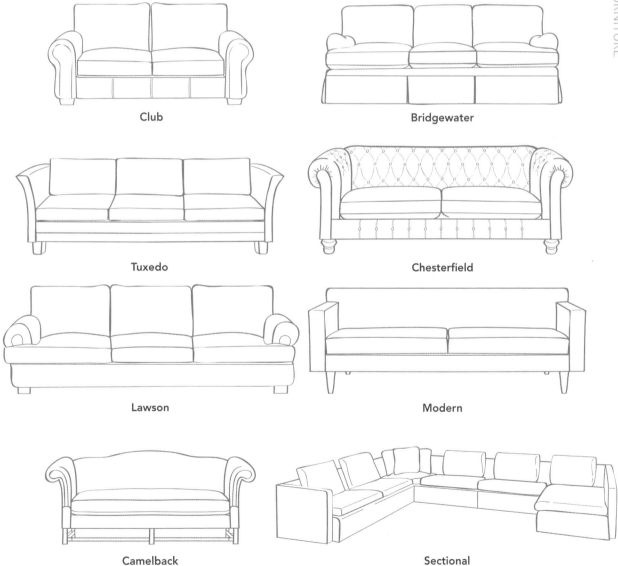

Club

Bridgewater

Tuxedo

Chesterfield

Lawson

Modern

Camelback

Sectional

MAKING ROOM FOR ENTERTAINMENT CENTERS

Whether placed in the family room or a living room, the entertainment center is a centerpiece that is almost more of a concept than a piece of furniture. Yes, you can purchase prefabricated units, but in my experience, these large pieces can overwhelm the space, and it seems like a universal law that clutter increases to fill the available space. I avoid these prefab pieces and instead use wall-mounted TVs whenever possible, with wall-mounted or free-standing shelves sized to suit the electronics you own. This creates a much cleaner, streamlined appearance. It can also save you money, because detailed entertainment centers with all the bells and whistles can be budget eaters.

Match comfortable seating to the TV, and position it with a good view of the screen. If I have the available floor space, I'll include a secondary seating group with a coffee table to create a nonvideo play and relaxation area. Sometimes it's good to remind ourselves that not every activity revolves around the TV.

the furniture of food

With your relaxation, socializing, and entertainment areas under control, it's time to tackle the rooms where food is the focus. Food means a lot to my family, and I think that's true of most families. The best kitchens and dining rooms are about preparing, sharing, eating, and enjoying good food and good company. So my rule for the kitchen and dining room is: Furnish to enrich the experience.

By that I mean the furniture in these rooms should make it easy to serve a meal, easy to eat it, and easy to clean up afterward. That way, the importance is on enjoying meals rather than trying to struggle around a cramped table. If people linger in a kitchen or dining room long after the meal is over, it's a sign that the room's design is a success.

The same clean, white shelving-and-cabinet units are used for the entertainment center and elsewhere in this funky family room, lending visual stability to an eclectic mix of furniture styles, colors, and textures.

A stunning island sits in the middle of a dynamic layout in this contemporary kitchen. The positions of all the elements make this an inviting space in which to cook and eat.

The kitchen has become the social hub of the modern home. People can often be found sitting around a kitchen table even between meals. As they socialize, do homework, or play games—as families increasingly do at the kitchen table—they sprawl. So it's really important to leave room for people to skew their chairs at angles to have conversations with someone preparing food, or smoothly rise from the table.

Although there are plenty of options among tables and chairs for the kitchen or dining room, you can often update an old table with a new coat of paint or by refinishing it—as long as the shape and size work in the room's layout. Round tables are the most common shape for kitchens (the shape leaves everyone at the table facing everyone else, creating a wonderful social dynamic), while rectangular is the most common shape for dining room tables (leaves the most space for food in the center of the table). Really, though, use a shape

that conforms best to the shape of the room. For instance, let's say your dining room is square and you're already using round or oval coffee tables, occasional tables, and nightstands in other rooms. A round dining room table would probably work well with the shape of the room and would maintain design continuity from room to room.

I prefer expandable tables for both kitchen and dining room. Being able to change the size of the table gives you a lot of flexibility in arranging for different seating. Sideboards and hutches are popular dining room additions, and these pieces are often sold as a suite in combination with the table and chairs. As I've discussed, include these secondary pieces only when there is sufficient space and a real need for the extra storage. A dining room limited to a nice light fixture over an attractive table and chairs can make a very strong, elegant impression. If you absolutely must use a secondary piece, corner units or skinny console tables are the most space efficient.

This handsome dark-wood dining table partners with simple and elegant chairs, creating a focal point in the room. The key, though, is that the table is perfectly sized for the space, allowing for comfortable dining and easy navigation around the table.

The simple glass-topped kitchen table leaves plenty of room for movement, and the cabinets and matching shelves supply all the storage—and snazzy looks—that the homeowner could want. No secondary pieces required.

I feel the same about a kitchen. It doesn't need much more than a table and chairs, perhaps some stools, and of course, cabinetry. Usually, you'll be designing around the existing cabinetry, but in the case of a large remodeling project, new cabinets may be in the budget.

If you're in the market for new cabinets, the first choice will be between *face frame* and *frameless*. Frameless cabinets are a box; the doors rest inside the front edge of the box or are mounted on the outside, covering the edges. Frameless cabinets are a more European, less formal, and less traditional look, one that would be right at home in a sleek contemporary kitchen or a modern design.

Face frame cabinets have a frame attached to the front of the cabinet box, like a picture frame. The door can be mounted to sit inside the frame or, more commonly, it's mounted in front of the frame.

The framing style sets the tone of the cabinet. Doors on a frameless cabinet are usually flat or very plain, while those on face frame cabinets are often detailed. Wood and wood veneer are used to craft both types, and you'll find cabinets in a full spectrum of stains from blond to ebony. However, frameless cabinets are often offered in easy-to-clean laminates as well. As a general rule, if you want colored cabinets for your kitchen, you'll be looking at frameless.

Consider glass fronts for new cabinets. Glass fronts come plain, but you can also dress them up with bevels or even choose stained-glass inserts. Regardless, I use glass fronts on only a few cabinets—those with the prettiest dishware and glasses inside.

One last thought for when you're considering the number and layout of your new cabinets. I've found that open shelving can be a fantastic low-cost and beautiful complement to kitchen cabinetry. If you have a lot of stunning serving plates and stemware, using open shelving will embellish the overall look of your kitchen. I think too often homeowners automatically assume that installing new cabinets means covering all available wall space with

sabrina's tip

ABOUT FACE

Save money by refacing rather than replacing older cabinets. Whether you hire professionals or handle the job yourself, the process is the same. Veneer or laminate panels are glued to the cabinet fronts, and doors are refinished, resurfaced, or replaced. Combined with sparkling new hardware and a thorough cleaning inside and out, refacing can create a whole new look at a fraction of the cost of brand-new cabinets.

They may look brand-new, but these cabinets were revived with refacing rather than replacement. The glass mosaic tile is part of a clean, fresh, stylish look.

cabinetry. Don't fall into that trap—turn to shelving for striking kitchen displays.

No discussion of kitchen furniture is complete without touching on islands. Your kitchen

Top: Flat-faced ebony cabinets set the tone for this sleek kitchen design that features stainless-steel countertops and exquisite pendant lights over the island.

Bottom: An interesting mix of cabinet fronts livens up the look of this kitchen. Ribbed glass keeps what's stored inside (kind of) a mystery, while metallic laminate on other cabinet fronts adds even more visual interest.

may include a built-in island that only needs to be updated—painted or refaced—to work beautifully in your new design. Sometimes, though, a kitchen has a wide-open space without an island. In those cases, think about adding one for both functional and aesthetic reasons.

Islands are available as both free-standing and mobile units. Free-standing islands are usually the more physically substantial option, often built with drawers or cabinets. Rolling islands, on the other hand, are usually built with an open construction that incorporates shelves or racks. Either type comes in a bounty of materials and styles that can be matched to your kitchen cabinetry, table, or accents like hanging pot racks. Whichever you choose, base your decision on the need for extra prep space and storage and the desire to add a visual element to a blank spot in the kitchen layout.

furnishing private spaces

Bedrooms are sanctuaries where we are at our most intimate. The choice of furniture has to

This kitchen features a stunning island with room for four seats and a beautiful engineered-stone countertop—and plenty of prep space for the cook!

A simple, well-appointed kitchen is well served by a wide island topped with a wonderful distressed walnut-plank countertop. Two cushy stools ensure that the diners' side of the island is as comfortable as it is attractive.

Sometimes an unbalanced design works. This asymmetrical platform bed includes a handy side table, and the lopsided design provides the basis for the room's look. As this bedroom clearly shows, beds are usually the dominant centerpiece in a bedroom.

reflect and respect that. That's why my rule for bedrooms is: Reinforce intimacy and luxury. This may seem a little broad, but let's start with the centerpieces to see how it works in practice.

First off, you're going to spend a third or more of your life on your bed and mattress; shouldn't they both be of superior quality? If that means replacing that thirty-year-old mattress and ugly steel bed frame that came with it, so be it.

APPEALING BED STYLES

Mattresses are about comfort; beds are all about setting the design style of the bedroom. However, the bed you choose must also work with the bedroom's relatively simple layout. I always use a bedroom's size to determine how ornate a bed can be. A bed should never crowd the room. For illustrated examples of the following bed styles, see page 128.

- **Platform.** This streamlined style is gaining in popularity with the growth in sales of memory-foam mattresses that require solid support surfaces. Platform beds are just that: a basic, flat platform. Some come unadorned, while others include headboards that may include storage such as bookshelves or just back rests. The platform itself can mirror the size of the

mattress or be designed with an extended lip all the way around the bed. Keep in mind that the bigger the lip and the deeper the headboard, the more room the bed will need.

I find that platforms are best suited to modern and contemporary bedrooms, although honestly, the styles within the platform construction cover a lot of looks. Storage beds are a common variation with drawers, shelves, or cabinets below the platform. They can be a great choice for adding storage to a bedroom. Platform beds are also often lower than beds with box springs; be sure to take the height into account when choosing side tables.

- **Sleigh.** The name comes from the curvy headboard and footboard that give the bed the appearance of an old-fashioned, horse-drawn sleigh. Sleigh beds are a substantial style, sturdy and large. The bed requires adequate space, not only to accommodate hefty physical proportions, but also to ensure that the weighty visual appearance doesn't overwhelm the look of the bedroom.

- **Canopy.** This lovely style was first used in royal bedrooms, where wraparound heavy curtains provided an extra barrier against drafty castles. The bed looks best in a room with high ceilings, and few beds can rival the dramatic look. The frame includes four corner posts that support a top frame, echoing the bed frame. The headboard and footboard, if any, are usually modest. The framework is traditionally draped with fabric that determines the overall look, as much as the material used to construct the frame. A gauzy wrap of silk or linen creates a light and airy feel that definitely tends toward the feminine.

- **Poster.** Capturing the vertical elegance of a canopy bed, a poster bed comes with legs that extend upward at each corner of the bed into posts. The traditional *four-poster* is outfitted with tall, decoratively shaped posts. The style can be just a frame and posts, or it may include simple head and foot rails or more decorative treatments. Either way, this is a period style that has been adapted to just about every contemporary look—from the thin, clean lines of Shaker, to ornamental iron, to sharp stainless-steel modern versions. *Cannonball* beds are a chunkier variation, with shorter posts topped with finials meant to resemble cannonballs. You'll find a style of poster bed will work as long as the ceiling is high enough for the posts on the bed you choose.

- **Traditional.** This is one of the most widely used bed styles, comprised of a basic metal frame with a decorative headboard and footboard. The frame serves as a foundation for a box spring and mattress set. The headboard and footboard set the style, and you'll find versions in all kinds of woods, wrought iron, and upholstery. Because there as so many different styles, The style suits just about any type of bedroom. It's also a fairly compact construction, so it works in smaller bedrooms.

Of course, cost is always an issue, right? That's partly why I'm fond of using platform beds—the look is clean and works with a boatload of decorative styles, and it saves you the cost of a box spring.

The right nightstand complements the style of the bed, as this one does admirably. To choose a bedside table lamp, the bottom of your lamp should be the same height of your chin when you're sitting on your bed. The light should illuminate your reading material and not be too distracting.

ORDER IN THE BEDROOM

Nightstands are your bed's partners, and come in the similar diversity of styles. You may have purchased your nightstands as a set with the bed, but there's nothing stopping you from spiffing them up with a new finish or coat of paint and different drawer pulls. If you have your heart set on new nightstands, keep in mind they should match the style of the room and bed.

Nightstands are a great way to experiment with a slightly more adventurous look. I've seen people use small tree trunks, stacked up blocks of wood, and even metal gym lockers. As long as they serve the purpose, fit the space, and complement the decor, take a chance!

You might be surprised that I consider the dresser a secondary piece in the bedroom. With closet systems becoming less expensive and offering amazing accessories, it's easy to outfit a medium

or large closet with all the customized storage you'll need. I also think that putting pretty sweaters on a wall-mounted shelf can make them part of the decor. There's lot of storage alternatives, and that's why I just don't believe dressers are always necessary, or even preferable, in every bedroom. At the end of the day, if you decide to use one, make absolutely sure it doesn't impede traffic flow in the bedroom. As with most other furniture, don't hesitate to paint or stain your current dresser and change the hardware to update the look and make it work better with the room's decor.

Where floor space allows, I like to include a small bench or chest at the foot of the bed. You'd be surprised at how handy it is to have a stable surface on which to sit down and put on socks or stockings and shoes. A bench also provides a place to put a folded blanket or afghan, while a chest serves as excellent concealed, easy-access, seasonal storage for extra bed linens, winter sweaters, and more.

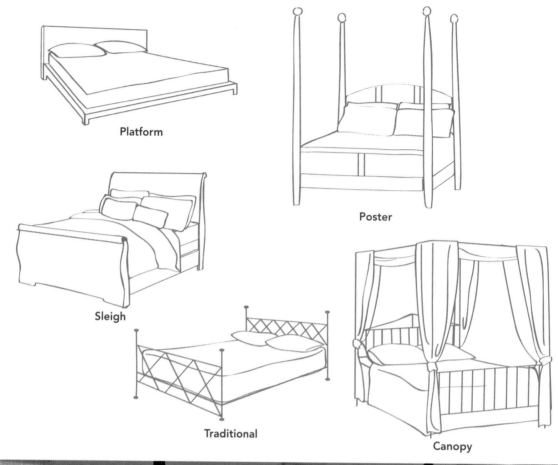

Platform

Poster

Sleigh

Traditional

Canopy

A basic bench not only provides a decorative flourish, but also is a handy surface for sitting while dressing.

The beauty of this twins' nursery—besides the spectacular color scheme—is that most everything can be repurposed as the children grow. Although the cribs will be handed off to other parents, the dresser can be painted or stained for future use, the closet system can be reconfigured, and the rocker can be repainted or left as is to do duty on the porch.

tidy kids' spaces

Kids also need their version of a sanctuary, a bedroom that reflects their personality and where they feel like the space is all theirs. My rule for children's bedrooms is: Prepare for change, because that's a constant with children. Because of this, I always look to furnish a child's bedroom with convertible pieces that will hold up to being refinished or painted multiple times. For instance, use stacking bunk beds for your adolescent son, and when he reaches his teen years, lose the upper bunk and refinish or paint the bottom bed for an updated, hipper look.

I find that it helps to get kids involved in the process of decorating their rooms. I like to have them pick colors and design features whenever possible and reasonable. I even let them chime in on the choice of furniture. The nightstand is a perfect example.

Usually, a child needs only one, and you can balance your son or daughter's tastes against longevity. Use a solid wood or metal unit and you can change the finish—paint or stain—or other details rather than replace the piece in later years.

Most secondary pieces in a kid's bedroom are all about storage. Chests, simple wood shelves, and wicker or wood baskets can all be adapted over time to grow with the room's occupant.

a workable design

There's one other personal space that often gets overlooked in the process of editing furniture, and that's the home office. Regardless of where you put it, the big rule for furnishing a home office is: Integrate seamlessly. This means looking for a desk, chair, and other furniture that blends in.

A comfortable and stylish chair goes hand-in-glove with a fold-down melamine desk surface in this brightly colored bedroom. The desk provides lots of room to work, and the shelves include hidden storage for work-related essentials. As a bonus, the panel over the desk drops down to reveal a bunk bed for guests.

sabrina's tip

THE REACH-IN OFFICE

If you absolutely have no space for a home office, a closet can easily be transformed into one. I had to do this in my first apartment, and it cost me only about $50. For an inexpensive desk, I bought a hollow-core door and finished it with several coats of polyurethane that I tinted with artists' pigment. I mounted the door inside the closet, on tiny metal L brackets I found at the hardware store. A secondhand rolling editor's chair completed my work-area furnishings and the chair tucked neatly under my homemade desk when I wanted work to disappear.

Generally, you don't need it to make a design statement. I focus most of my attention on finding the right desk. It has to be large enough to accommodate whatever work is done there, but should also fit appropriately into the space provided by the room's layout (preferably not facing a wall, but floating in the space).

There are lots of period style or even contemporary desks that bring some flair to what is inevitably a functional space. First and foremost, choose a style that holds everything you need. You'll even find types with specialized drawers for holding things like printers and hanging files, and special channels to contain cables.

With your furniture edited, you're probably starting to really see that design vision you described in your Design Journal finally beginning to take shape. At this point, the "bones" of your interior design are in place, and now it's time add the "skin." That means diving into the wonderful world of textiles.

the sixth layer

select your textiles

Pleasing to the touch and a delight to the eye, textiles can be incredibly powerful pieces of your new design. They make specific areas of a room stand out as beautiful stopping points for the eye and inviting surfaces for the hand. As beautiful as they can be, designing with fabrics is first and foremost an exercise in texture. The surface texture will determine how the color reads and will account for much of the visual and tactile interest. The texture can even have an impact on a room's mood. Smooth or sheer fabrics add a clean, cool and sophisticated vibe. The softness and visible weave of linen or cotton sets a less formal, cozier, and warmer tone.

In choosing the fabric with the look you want, keep durability in mind. Drapes are constantly being opened and closed, rugs are walked on, bedding nestles us while we sleep, and upholstery is subjected to the wear and tear of sitting, reclining, and sprawling bodies. A fabric's life is a tough one, made even tougher if you have a busy home or one full of kids and pets. That's no truer than for upholstery.

fab textiles

Fabrics can be broken down into two main groups: *synthetics* and *naturals*. Synthetics tend to be more durable, easier to keep clean, and less expensive. Natural fabrics are usually more appealing to touch and are more unique, with surface variations that synthetics can't completely copy. Your ideal fabric may lie somewhere in between; natural and synthetic fibers are regularly blended in fabrics that capture the best of both worlds.

silk

Silk is all about luster. Shimmering in unbelievably vibrant colors, this sensual material makes for jaw-dropping drapery. On the other hand, upholster furniture in silk and you create a very delicate

surface. Silk upholstery is best on pieces that will serve a largely decorative rather than a practical role. Silk is also a fantastic choice for beautiful accents, such as a dining table runner. However, not all silk is created equal. Although any type can be a little pricey, raw silk has irregularities in both color and surface texture that make it a less expensive version (although many people, including me, find the imperfections enchanting). The finest silks, such as Italian dupioni or Thai silks, boast deep and amazingly rich colors. The material is also treated and fabricated in lots of ways, such as silk charmeuse (a stiff version that is regularly backed with crepe) and brocade, an embossed version.

cotton and linen

I talk about these fabrics together because they look a lot alike and both are offered in solid colors, white, and prints. You'll find both used widely in drapery and upholstery, but cotton is the fabric of choice for bedding. Durable and lovely to the touch, these are also some of the most reasonably priced fabrics. Cotton and linen are even blended together, creating tough, handsome, and soft upholstery or drapery. Cotton and cotton blends are used in slipcovers. Both of these natural fabrics are susceptible to shrinkage and staining (they are often chemically treated

Previous page: The robin's egg blue drapes in this living room complement the wall covering, and the solid color of the window panels helps break up the expanse of patterned surface.

to combat those problems). They are naturally beautiful and offer a more subtle look than other fabrics. I find that either of these works great in just about any design style, and can find a spot in every room of the house.

wool

The quintessential natural fiber, wool is incredibly durable, naturally stain-resistant, and easy on the eyes. Wool upholstery and floor coverings are tough enough to hold up to heavy use, and wool can be woven in a number of different textures and patterns and dyed just about any color. Whatever the look, wool makes for a warm surface.

leather and suede

Genuine animal hide is one of the most durable upholstery materials. Match your decor with stains from light brown through black, or turn to pigmented leather in deep, rich colors such as purple and red. Unlike the rest of us, leather gets better looking with age. Marks of wear and tear only make the surface more handsome, and the finish deepens and mellows over time. It is also extremely easy to clean. Suede has a short, dense nap that feels almost like velvet and has to be treated to prevent staining. Suede makes for long-lasting upholstery that would look spectacular in a contemporary or even a traditional interior.

This intimate seating area features a stunning mix of textures and colors. The settee and chair are covered in a scintillating cut velvet, while the chair boasts a lovely lavender ultrasuede that complements the silver block leaf finish on the arms.

synthetics

Some awfully nice fabrics come out of the lab. High-end synthetics are used in handsome, inexpensive window treatments and upholstery, but they are often combined with natural fibers such as cotton to make a durable fabric with a nice feel at a low cost. You'll find synthetics in tons of colors and patterns.

- **Nylon** is the king of synthetics: extremely durable, pleasant to the touch, wrinkle-resistant, and largely fade-proof.
- **Polyester** runs a close second; it is UV-resistant, washable, and has a silky-smooth surface (although pure polyester fabrics tend to pill, forming small balls under repeated contact).
- **Acrylic** is the wool imitator of this group, with the same soft feel and fire and stain resistance (although it, too, has a tendency to pill).
- **Acetate** is a low-cost alternative that looks convincingly like silk and maintains an attractive flowing shape when used to make drapes. Appealingly soft, it is easily damaged by sun exposure.
- **Rayon** is more delicate than acetate, with a look that rivals satin but a body that will wrinkle and shrink if not properly cared for.

velvet

Velvet can be created using any fiber; prices vary based on the fiber used. The secret behind velvet's enchanting texture is a distinctive method of weaving and manufacture that creates a dense, almost fuzzy pile. It's a magnet for the fingers, at once soft, rich, sumptuous, and warm. It absorbs light and sound as well. Velvet's colors are deep and exceedingly rich. It makes for dramatic drapes and, less often, soft upholstery with a distinctive look. However, if you have your heart set on a purple velvet couch, who am I to judge? Just keep an eye out for pieces that have been treated for stain resistance and are made from durable fiber blends, because velvet is generally prone to wear and is hard to clean.

vinyl

Vinyl is an economical choice for upholstery, with surface textures from perfectly smooth to raised grain that imitates leather. It's also available in many colors, easy to clean, and essentially waterproof. It can, however, crack over time when exposed to strong sun, and small cuts and scratches can easily turn into tears. It's not a luxury feel, and I wouldn't cover a whole living room suite in the stuff, but there are situations perfectly suited for vinyl's personality. I use it wherever durability and cleanability outweigh the need for a lavish, warm surface. For instance, I wouldn't hesitate to cover chrome chair frames in vinyl to go around a centerpiece throwback Formica kitchen table in a retro kitchen.

microfiber

This relative newcomer is an innovative use of synthetic fibers. Made of polyester or polymers, microfiber material is constructed of (as you might have guessed from the name) extremely small fibers. The manufacturing process produces a surface texture that convincingly imitates suede. Microfiber upholstery comes in a full palette of colors, from sophisticated to, well, not so much. I'm not entirely sold on using microfiber fabric in every room in the house, but the material can make a nice furniture covering. The big selling point is that almost anything can be cleaned off of microfiber.

Fabrics are a designer's dream: the perfect combination of enchanting texture, vivid color, and fabulous patterns.

That makes it perfect for a sofa in a busy family room where snacks are ever-present, or on a chair in a kid's room that sees its share of arts and crafts activities.

When it comes to repurposing upholstered furniture, there are two ways to go: Use a slipcover or reupholster an existing piece. The option you choose depends on both design and budget considerations.

dressing your furniture

As lovely as wood or steel might be, cover a sofa or chair in fabric and you add a whole new dimension to the piece. I'm betting you've walked into a room where the upholstery just wowed you. Fabric can be design magic. It doesn't matter if you're looking for a surface to be a focal point or just want a nice texture as a great supporting player for other pieces in the design. However you use it, upholstery determines to a large extent how comfortable the room will feel.

slipcovers

Revive a couch or chair inexpensively with a slipcover. Although they don't rival upholstery, slipcovers can provide a clean new appearance for a piece you can't afford to (or don't want to) reupholster. They come in several different fabrics, and you can find them in solids and patterns, with nice features such as piping or tassels. Judge the durability of a slipcover the same way you would upholstery: by the type of fabric and protective treatments for stain and water resistance.

A mix of upholstery materials adds to a texture-rich living room that boasts a distinctive rug and simple drapes. The scene is kept under control with muted colors; matching arm panels and throw pillows add a splash of pattern to the mix.

sabrina's tip

THE CAUTIOUS APPROACH TO FABRIC PATTERNS

Many of my clients get a little nervous at the idea of committing to a patterned sofa or chair fabric. I don't blame them; patterns can overwhelm a space and it's not always clear how well they'll work over time, or how quickly they'll become dated. That doesn't mean you have to do entirely without pattern. You can try out interesting splashes of pattern in the form of pillows or patterned throws draped over the back of a sofa. It's a great way to put your toe in the water.

The keys to a slipcover looking good, as opposed to looking like a sheet draped over an old couch, are good fabric, a good fit, and great tucking. Also, before placing a slipcover over your old sofa, give it a good ironing (or you can mist it and place it in the dryer for a few minutes).

new fabric, new look

Reupholstering a beat-up, sub-par club chair doesn't make much sense if the frame is already compromised. You'll end up dumping that chair in couple of years, along with your still-fresh upholstery. On the other hand, if your current sofa fits your new layout perfectly and has the great bones of a solid-wood frame, screwed and glued together, you're probably buying yourself another decade of beautiful use with a new covering of fabric.

A clean, spare interior calls for minimal upholstered furnishings that stay true to the simple lines of the design. This sofa and chair are perfect for the room, with squared-off, firm cushions and solid colors that complement the room's design. Tufted cushions on the couch add restrained flair to a minimalist design approach.

Keep in mind that fabric is just one component of reupholstering. Most times, the process also involves adding padding, springs, or other guts that can contribute to the final cost. Get a complete estimate to truly judge whether it makes sense to reupholster.

choosing quality upholstery

So you've come to the conclusion that you want to go shopping for a new sofa or chair that suits the space—with lines that fit right into your design? Look for new upholstered pieces that are constructed to last (see tips for how to determine furniture quality in *The Fifth Layer: Edit Your Furniture*). Any retailer who sells quality furniture offers a number of different fabric options. If none of those options catches your eye, you can order custom upholstery for a (significant) bump in price.

Whether you're reupholstering or buying new, weigh your fabric choice against the needs of your design and the beating the piece will take. Will the upholstery be facing the rough and tumble of TV dinners and life in a well-used family room? If the answer is yes, you should probably limit your search to more durable fabrics that are easy to clean (or protected by a stain-resistance treatment like Scotchgard) and that will still look reasonably fresh after a few years of abuse. Look at finer fabrics, such as silk blends, if the chair is only used on special, formal occasions.

The "tell" of furniture upholstery quality is all in the details:

- Fabric patterns should match (designs line up, and large or bold figurals such as flowers aren't cut in half).
- Loose threads or buttons are a sure sign of sloppy upholstering.

Crisp lines, flawless seams, and smooth surfaces are all signs of high-quality upholstery, as the chairs in this contemporary dining room vividly illustrate.

Textile patterns mark this elegant living room's pieces. The understated pattern on the green chairs is just enough to provide interesting visual variation in an otherwise sedate room design.

- Pleats are a sign of high-end upholstery, and add flair as well as cost.
- The best fabrics have patterns woven into the material, not just printed on them.

If you're redoing a piece for a busy room, you might even want to look at commercial fabrics designed for hotels and institutional use.

Cushion filling determines seating comfort and longevity. Stay away from low-end, shredded-foam cushions because they lose their shapes quickly. "Foam-inside-fabric" is a common and durable mid-range construction, and durable polyester-wrapped foam is the next step up. Some cushions include down packed around a foam core, making for a soft, but not too soft, seat. Pure down cushions are considered the height of luxury, although some people aren't fans of sinking deep into a couch or chair. Down cushions also have to be regularly fluffed to maintain their attractive appearance.

I always nail down my upholstery decisions before choosing other fabrics for a room. The truth is that furniture fabric can dominate the view and is more of a foreground element in a room design. Still, I just love when it comes time to choose window treatments. That particular exercise combines the fun of diving into a bounty of fabrics with the creative challenge of matching form, length, and function. So let's look at what taking that plunge entails.

winning window veils

Ask five interior designers to define the difference between drapes and curtains, and you'll get at least five different explanations. So for the purposes of this discussion, a curtain is a lightweight window treatment that is usually unlined. I consider drapes heavier window treatments, just touching or puddling on the floor (not more than 3 inches). They are lined to protect

These plain, unpleated gray grommeted drapes may be simply hung, but they are the height of elegance.

against sun damage, block light transmission, and serve as a barrier to drafts. Lining also ensures drapes maintain an alluring form.

Inside these definitions, there are a million and one possibilities. Drapes and curtains can be hung alone or as part of a layered window treatment. They can be hung to different lengths and varying widths, can close completely or not at all, can be topped by valances or other treatments, and on and on. So let's try to make this easy.

I choose window treatments in a three-step process. First, I pick out the fabric that best suits the room, with colors and patterns that contribute to the design. Then I play around with hanging styles and different lengths, to find the most attractive look for the window. Finally, I embellish

THE LINGO OF TEXTILES

Whether you're on the hunt for the perfect sofa covering or looking for just the right panels to accent a picture window, you're going to stumble across a whole lot of fancy-sounding words on your journey. A modest fabric vocabulary will help you cut to the chase on your way to the perfect textile.

Warp and weft: Fibers that run lengthwise in a woven fabric are called the *warp*, while those that run perpendicular to the warp are called the *weft*.

Jacquard: Jacquard is a type of loom used to create fabrics with vivid floral, figural, or geometric patterns, including those with raised designs. Jacquard weaves include damask and brocade.

Damask: This reversible fabric weave usually features either stripes or floral designs where one section of the design is shiny and the other is not. It is a bit of a formal look, but a damask textile is a medium-weight fabric that can make stunning upholstery, drapes, and bedspreads.

Matelassé: A weave used with many different fibers, matelassé creates a quilted appearance, but has no padding in the fabric. This creates a heavy, dense fabric.

Sheer: Sheer fabrics are airy, pretty, and delicate. You can find sheer curtains with patterns, but that seems kind of beside the point to me; sheer panels should seem like color floating in the air—a pattern makes the treatment look heavier. The light appearance is also why sheer panels are often used in layered window treatments and never in upholstery.

Brocade: Similar to damask, a brocade weave features finer, more elegant patterns and is generally used with lighter weight or finer fibers such as silk. Brocade is used in high-end drapes, bedding, and upholstery. It's a formal or period look.

Chambray or chambric: This is a down-to-earth weave, usually using cotton. It's a lightweight country-style fabric, made from a warp of one color (traditionally blue), and a weft of another (traditionally white). The weave creates a soft, reasonably smooth surface that serves as durable, casual slipcovers and curtains.

Chenille: Describing both a fabric and the yarn used to make it, *chenille* is French for "caterpillar." This makes sense because the fabric is kind of fuzzy and soft. Chenille fabric is made from cotton or synthetics, usually in a solid color. It's used in upholstery, floor coverings, bedding, and drapery.

the look as appropriate, occasionally adding layers, and accents like tiebacks.

choosing panel length

Casual window treatment panels are usually hung to the sill, or the bottom of the windowsill's apron (especially if the bottom hem will show when light shines through the panel). Either length is informal and works well for a kitchen or a kid's room. More formal panels are hung to the bottom of the baseboard molding (just touching the floor). Some people prefer the more dramatic effect of *puddling* drapes—allowing 3 inches. As a general

rule, operable drapes are not puddled because the drape tail will collect dust from the floor surface every time the drapes are opened or closed.

I puddle drapes when I want to achieve a specifically romantic tone in a formal room large enough that I can be sure no one will walk across the drape panels or move a chair over them. In any case, long drapes are an elegant look that is ideal for living rooms, stylish and luxurious bedrooms, formal dining rooms, and any room that features tall, dramatic windows. Window treatments should hang at least 4 inches higher than your window molding and touch the floor. They should never be shorter like high-water pants.

Sheer drapes let abundant light in while complementing a richly textured space such as this living room.

Left: Full-length drapes are a formal style perfectly suited to a stylish formal dining room such as this. The unlined drapes allow a good deal of light in, to brighten the small space, and the drapes feature a center panel that ties in with the overall neutral color scheme.

sabrina's tip

FULL-LENGTH DRAMA

Looking for maximum excitement in your window treatments? Here's a way to add ceiling-to-floor drapes that hang like stage curtains. Use hospital curtain tracks installed along the ceiling right above the window. Hang your drapes from the ceiling all the way down to the bottom of the baseboard molding. It's a stunning look for a dining room, living room, or bedroom that needs a dash of panache.

Drapes can be a great way to deal with irregular shaped openings like the eyebrow windows over the French doors in this well-appointed and eclectic living room. The drapes cover the entire wall, blocking the view at night and creating a beautiful and elegant surface.

sabrina's rule

CONCEAL WINDOW FLAWS

Curtains and drapes aren't just window dressing; they can also be fixers, hiding imperfections in the windows themselves.

- **Odd-sized windows on the same wall.** Measure the panels for the largest window, and replicate that window treatment for all the windows. This will create a more unified and pleasing visual arrangement.
- **Skinny-window complex.** Where a window is noticeably narrow, mount wide panels on either side. It will create the illusion of a wider window.
- **Short or small window.** A short window can be made to appear taller by using long panels.
- **Undesirable view.** Make the most of your sun exposure while limiting that scenic view of your neighbor's garbage cans by hanging a sheer panel over the window, behind the curtain or drape panels.

Lining any drapery panel—regardless of style—adds and maintains the form of the panel.

- **Standard or regular lining** is a mid-weight blend of cotton and polyester.
- **Blackout liner** is just that, meant to stop all light from entering. It has a rubber texture and is relatively heavy. I'd use it in a bedroom that receives strong morning light or in a room with an upscale home theater.
- **Interlining** is commonly used between drapery fabric and a standard lining. It resembles flannel and supports the structure of drapery, as well as ensures that the lining's color doesn't show through the fabric panel in front.
- **Classic napped lining** performs both roles, preventing sun damage and show-through, and preserving the form of the fabric.

How you hang draperies plays a huge part in how they look. Curtains and some styles of drapes are slid onto the curtain rod, or hung by hardware attached to the back of the fabric panel. These styles are simply slid open or closed.

Always bring along a swatch of the window treatment fabric when you pick out a curtain rod.

Decorative poles and finials can dress up the look quite a bit. Rods and poles come in metal, wood, and plastic, in just about every finish imaginable, and diameters from thin to thick. Finials include simple balls or end caps and much more detailed fixtures that complement formal fabrics and designs. Always bring along a swatch of the window treatment fabric when you pick out a curtain rod. More formal drapes are fitted with special hangers that ride in tracks, allowing the panels to be opened or closed with a single pull cord. Your metal finish should match your decor. Traditional rooms can be brushed antique brass

or oil-rubbed bronze, for a more contemporary room, opt for brushed nickel, steel, or chrome.

the blinds and shades story

No matter what they're made of, blinds and shades serve the same function as curtains and drapes. Like fabric panels, they can be hung alone or as part of a layered window treatment.

- **Roller shades.** The plain Jane of window coverings, roller shades are basic fixtures with an opaque or semi-opaque sheet that rolls and unrolls. Even though you'll find modern versions in colorful variations of the traditional cream or white, roller shades are still pretty simple. I use them as either a single window treatment or with other accessories as part of a layered look. Most roller shades are made of a stiff, papery material coated in a semi-gloss finish. High-end versions come with motorized controls.

- **Cellular shades.** Also called *honeycomb shades*, these are made of a series of collapsible "cells." The cells act as insulators that keep heat and air conditioning in, and sound out. Cellular shades are offered in a limited selection of colors, with off-white being the most popular. I like to use them in modern or streamlined contemporary decors. *Pleated shades* are the poorer cousin to cellular shades. Don't get me wrong, they look every

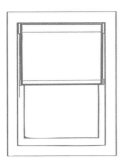

Roller shade

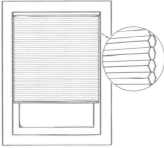

Cellular shade

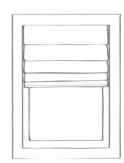

Roman shade

bit as nice as cellular types. They just don't have the extra insulation value.

- **Roman shades.** Formed of vertical panels that overlap when closed, roman shades are a terrific look by themselves. They're available in the same vast selection of fabrics you'd find in shopping for drapes. They are also easy to install and simple to use, with a pull-cord mechanism that raises and lowers the panels. Given the exceptional variety among roman shades, I'd use them with confidence in any room of the house.

- **Standard blinds.** When you're looking to quickly and easily add basic window coverings to a utility room, guest bedroom, or other understated interior space, you'll find that plain horizontal blinds are real budget savers. They are, however, not a distinctive look. Made in vinyl or aluminum, they feature rows of thin, horizontal panels that can be opened in position with a simple crank handle to moderate light exposure, or pulled completely open with a pull cord. I use these as a default in areas like a kid's bedroom that is the arena for rough play. You won't mind if they take a beating. Mini-blinds are a somewhat more stylish version that I would use in a kitchen or sitting room.

- **Venetian blinds.** In reality, all slatted blinds can be called Venetian blinds, because the term describes blinds with operable slats. However, in the design world, "Venetian blinds" describes an upscale product, usually

made of wood slats connected with wide, decorative fabric or tape. These can be really stylish; stained light, medium, or dark; and with coordinated or contrasting fabric bands. Venetian blinds are operated the same way standard blinds are, but the decorative impact is much greater. I prefer to use true Venetian blinds all by themselves in a slightly informal or casual room—especially a study or man's bedroom. But that's not to say they wouldn't look great coupled with solid-colored, simple drapes or curtains.

choosing your window treatment

Choosing the perfect window treatment for your room and your windows is a matter of balancing practical considerations against your aesthetic goals. Be realistic about light exposure. I don't care how beautiful sheer bedroom curtains might be; if they don't block strong, direct morning light, they're not the right window treatment for the room. Also honestly consider the wear and tear the room will see. You'd be surprised how much abuse window treatments can take in a rambunctious family room or a kids' room shared by two brothers. Nothing makes a room look quite as sad as truly timeworn drapes or curtains.

Match the total window treatment to your design style. If you're all about a simple, spare aesthetic, stick to drapes, curtains, or blinds used alone. More formal or involved room designs open the door to more complex window treatments. Where your room is developing a full-throttle personality, don't be afraid to layer a window treatment. Start from the base, such as a sheer panel over the window or sheer under-curtains, and build out from there. That way, you can easily check that each successive layer works with the previous one. Complete the look of your windows and you're ready to put rugs in place.

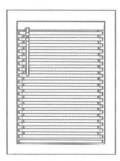

Standard blinds

Venetian blinds

Right: This modest rug not only allows the floor to be the star of the room, but it also visually ties together the furnishings in a small, cozy relaxation area.

amazing area rugs

I have one major unbreakable rule when it comes to floor coverings: Absolutely no rugs on rugs. So if you're sporting wall-to-wall carpeting throughout the home, you can just skip this section. You know you have the right rug when it looks like it's been there forever. There's no denying that a bold area rug can call attention to itself, but the best rugs seamlessly integrate into the whole look of the room. In my experience working with scads of homeowners, I've found that rugs are one of the key decorative elements that just get overlooked. As a designer, it's one of those common flaws that jumps out at me when I walk into a room—a big, bare floor with nothing tying furniture groupings together. Don't make that mistake.

Portable floor coverings usually have a place in every room of the house. An area rug often completes a layout, visually de... areas of a room. Most rugs are not ... busters, so there's not much excuse for ... without. The available designs and styles are ... varied that you'll find something perfect for your tastes and the room that you're decorating.

Start your search by size and shape. Area rugs come in several standard sizes (almost all are rectangles). You've already chosen furniture positions—at least on a sketch—so use that placement to determine the best rug size. An area rug in an entryway just needs to look good, suit the size and shape of the space, and be durable and washable. In most other rooms of the house, area rugs will anchor a piece of furniture or a furniture group. The rug under a conversation area with chairs and a sofa is usually organized so that all pieces sit within the borders of the rug. However, chairs are sometimes placed half on and half off

SABRINA SO

THE SIXT...

145

planning different
budget
...ding

... ule

... RUG
... TABLE!

... out dining room tables:
... ould be at least 26 inches
... the table. This ensures that
... he back legs of their chairs on
... of the rug.

I determine optimal rug size by sketching borders on top of the master floor plan sketch, or actually laying out the best borders using blue painter's tape. Either way, work from the dimensions of those borders to the closest standard rug size. Sometimes no standard size will meet your need; not to worry, you can order rugs custom-made to your specifications. Carpet stores actually do this all the time with carpet remnants that are cut to size and edge-bound for use as a rug.

the rug. It's a casual, informal look. If you like the look, make sure that all the furniture is placed half on, half off. Either way, rugs are excellent ways to pull together a particular area—whether it's the couch, coffee table, and chairs in front of a home theater setup, or the bed in a bedroom.

There should be an 18-inch buffer between the edge of the rug and any walls.

The area rug under this dining room table and chairs not only complements the neutral color scheme, but it is also perfectly sized so that the chairs don't touch the floor even when pulled out.

Regardless of the area you're trying to outline with the rug, most designers agree that there should be an 18-inch buffer between the edge of the rug and any walls. The obvious exception would be any small space with a small area rug, such as a modest entry vestibule. Beyond maintaining the buffer, the general rule is "the larger the room, the larger the area rug." Small rugs can get lost in a large space, and although you might be saving a little money, you're not helping your room design at all.

Rug placement is also important. Make sure that pathways through a room don't involve someone walking with one foot on the rug and the other on a bare surface. It's actually an off-putting feeling and leaves the impression that something is wrong with the room. I'm also mindful about where to position rugs under beds. I like to have at least 2 feet of rug sticking out from the edge of the bed on the sides and at the foot.

Even shopping within the confines of standard sizes, you're going to find an incredible diversity of options. A few can be costly, but most are reasonably priced. Ultimately, your choice should be driven by how well any rug complements the existing patterns, colors, and textures in the space.

arresting area rugs

Area rugs are some very useful additions to a room design. They can define spaces within a room, moderate the look and color of a floor, complement other textiles, and add their own patterns and textures to the design. Pick an area rug that works with the look you've chosen for your overall design.

PERSIANS AND ORIENTALS

Many people use these terms interchangeably because authentic Persian and Oriental rugs share hand-knotted construction, intricate

Look to match the rug's character to the room's style. A simple and informal pastel braided rug is the perfect addition to a bright nursery.

designs, dynamic colors, and unusually dense fiber piles that make the rugs durable and long lasting. The least expensive are machine-made reproductions widely available through retail carpet stores and home centers. The designs are intricate and ornate, focusing on floral, figural, or geometric patterns. I don't like to introduce a Persian or Oriental rug into a room full of busy patterns because the rug's design won't get the attention it deserves. However, in rooms decorated predominantly with solid-colored surfaces and features, the right Persian or Oriental rug can really shine. These rugs complement interiors from traditional to modern, and their rugged construction makes them a good choice even for fairly busy floor plans.

WOOL

Soft, durable, stain-resistant, and warm underfoot, wool makes for a luxurious area rug. Wool rugs also hold up well under heavy traffic and even stop static electricity in its tracks. You'll pay a bit more for wool, but you'll get a rug that looks beautiful and works with just about any decor. *Flokatis* are made of deliciously soft wool, woven through a wool backing to create a plush shag rug. I like the look for an eclectic or informal interior. Most flokati rugs are the attractive natural off-white color of the wool, although a small number are dyed in soft pastels.

NATURAL AND RENEWABLE FIBERS

Go green by choosing an area rug made of sisal, sea grass, jute, hemp, or bamboo. Depending on which natural material you choose, the texture can range from accommodating to downright rough. Whittle down your options based on whether you'll be walking barefoot on the rug. All of these rugs are reasonably durable and can serve in entryways, living rooms, and transition areas such as large hallways. The majority of natural fiber rugs are edged in a colored tape to preserve the structure of the rug and create a more polished look.

BRAIDED

You can cover your floor with a piece of Americana. Braided rugs are a traditional American floor covering, cozy, warm, and durable. Usually crafted in an oval shape, braided rugs come in all the colors of the rainbow. Different colors are usually speckled throughout the rug courtesy of the braiding process. No matter what color you choose, braided rugs are a very casual look that relates specifically to country-style interiors. I might use one in a funky or eclectic interior or under the table in a cottage-style kitchen, but I would not try to force the rug into a more contemporary or modern room design.

SYNTHETICS

The same processes used to make carpeting from synthetic fibers can turn out a tremendous assortment of area rug designs. Area rugs are made from the same fibers discussed in the third layer (see the "Carpet" section in *The Third Layer: Select Your Surface Treatments*), and because manufacturers have complete control over color and design, the rug styles can venture into, let's say, the truly bold. You can find solid-colored synthetic rugs, and even subdued neutrals to suit a more restrained color scheme. Synthetic rugs are generally durable and provide a nice soft surface to walk on (how soft depends, of course, on the specific fiber used). These rugs are also some of the least expensive.

One of the great things about rugs is that you can play around with their position after you get them home. Don't settle; find the exact right spot for a rug and it will add immeasurably to the room. Get the rugs settled and you can move on to choosing bed and bath textiles to finish this layer with style.

captivating linens and bedding

No discussion of textiles in room design would be complete without a nod to those hard-working fabrics that cover the bed and do double duty in the bathroom. It's easy to think of these textiles as something other than design elements. After all, they have to be there. We visually put them on par with our clothes, toothbrushes, and toilet paper.

That's a mistake. Bedding and other linens provide comfort and serve functional roles, but they are also strong visual pieces of the design puzzle in two often-smallish rooms in the house: the bathroom and the bedroom. Give them due consideration, the same as you would a rug or window treatment.

Textiles can be perfect for providing texture counterpoint in a room. The sumptuous upholstery and elegant floor-length drapes perfectly complement the wood table and bases, and metal chandeliers.

Bedding, especially, can be a design statement in and of itself. The problem I often have when I dive in to help a homeowner redesign her bedroom is that bedding lasts a long time, and people are reluctant to replace bedding that is in great shape just to spice up the look of a bedroom.

I understand that. It's why I get fancy with duvet covers, top blankets, and pillow shams. These are all easily swapped in and out to change up the look of a bedroom. I also like to set a neutral base with the sheets and pillowcases.

The bathroom presents even greater opportunities to jazz up the look with a few simple additions. I'm a bit of a clean freak, so I lean toward white towels, but that's me. Towels come in some spectacular jewel tones that bring a big splash of color and texture. Big, fluffy towels are not only a simple, inexpensive indulgence; they also provide visual relief from the many hard, high-gloss surfaces that most bathrooms present. The bathmat is a similar case. Choose one that matches the towels for a coordinated look, or pick a different material altogether, such as sea grass, to create another modest point of interest in the room. Have fun in

It doesn't get much more inviting than a crisply made bed with bright, clean bedding and tons of pillows. Accent pillows tie the bedding to the color scheme of this attic bedroom, but the look of the textiles beckons you to relax in comfort.

Hotel-quality towels should be shown off, not hidden. The sumptuous white towels on display in this bathroom provide textural contrast to the hard surfaces that define the space, adding a touch of luxury.

choosing these decorative elements. After all, you can change them pretty easily if the look doesn't grow on you.

The textiles in a room design really round out the look and make it richer and more complete. When you've worked your way through those decisions, you've come very close to finishing up your design. From here, all you have to do is light it appropriately and add some accents—which leads up to the seventh and eight layers, respectively.

the seventh layer

illuminate your design

Lighting is the most important element in interior design. Of course, not all light is the same. Hang a bare bulb in the middle of your room, and you'll begin to appreciate the nuances of light color, intensity, diffusion, and presentation. Exploiting all those nuances is the way to show your design to its best advantage.

Controlling light means understanding it. Interior design is affected by four types of light. There is sunlight (which itself varies from place to place, season to season, and according to exposure), along with three types of artificial light: ambient, task, and accent. I like to break ambient light down further into broad and fill lighting, but let's not put too fine a point on things just yet. For the moment, let's focus on natural light.

mastering the sun

Because most of us are not regularly at home during the day (and because we can't control sunlight the way we can artificial light), natural light plays less of a role in interior design than artificial light does—but it's still a very important role. You can take advantage of that role by understanding the room's exposure to sunlight.

You've already noted where natural light and shadow fall throughout the day on your floor plan sketch (see *The First Layer: Understand Your Space and Plan Your Design*). Chances are you checked the natural light during one short period. Unfortunately, natural light is a little more complex than that. First off, the sun sits lower in the sky in the winter and higher in the summer. That means you need to double-check the positioning of furniture and the placement of decorative elements.

For instance, if it's spring and you've positioned a semi-circle of chairs to take advantage of the stunning view out a picture window, you might find that in winter, the sun shines right into people's eyes. The same holds true for the position of televisions and computer monitors. Take some time to review your furniture layout and head off any seasonal lighting problems.

More often, though, the problem is too little rather than too much natural light. It's not unusual for people who have developed dark, dramatic interior designs to find that the room seems a bit cavelike during the day. This can even happen in a room with a mid-range color scheme and an abundance of matte, light-absorbing surfaces. Whatever the case, a space that's overly dark during the day is the opposite of welcoming. I've found that the solution usually involves a few simple strategies. A healthy trimming of light-filtering foliage from trees and shrubs close to the house often does the trick. You may need to go a step further and modify overly cumbersome window treatments that are blocking more light than they should. Further amplify natural light in any space by adding a few strategically placed mirrors and introducing decorative accents with highly reflective surfaces.

Most times, even one of these changes can make all the difference. When you're confident that you've done all you can with the natural light the space receives, it is time to create your artificial lighting plan for the room.

Previous page: Low-voltage cables can be installed when existing junction boxes are in an awkward corner of the room. This kitchen features modern halogen pendants that are hung from a cable system and ample nature light, effectively combining the best of both types of lighting.

The design in a sun-washed space like this living room should account for exposure. Fade-proof fabrics, dark colors, and absorbent textures are all at home in a sunny room.

the grand lighting plan: artificial light

No matter what room or space you're designing, lighting should never be a haphazard affair. Room lighting has to promote safety, accommodate all the activities the space was designed for, and create the mood you envisioned for the space. That's a lot to ask. Nailing all those goals requires a methodical approach and a well-thought-out plan.

Lighting plans involve layers. I always start with the overarching ambient lighting, because how well ambient light penetrates throughout the space will determine what type of task and accent lighting you'll need to add.

There are really two types of ambient light. *General* ambient light disperses throughout a room, creating areas of light and shadow. Smaller ambient light fixtures, such as table lamps, provide *fill* lighting that supplements the main ambient light source and banishes shadows.

Many rooms already have a main wired-in fixture, such as an overhead flush-mount light or a chandelier in a dining room. Start there. How well does the light from that fixture penetrate into corners? Does anything block the light? Are there specific areas that require more intense lighting for activities such as reading or food preparation? Pencil in these notes on your floor plan sketch (see page 8).

Next, mark the areas that need fill lighting. These areas may be relatively far from the main ambient light source, or they may be spaces where light is blocked by a piece of furniture or an architectural feature such as a column. Fill lighting is also traditionally used where a small amount of more intense light is helpful but not necessarily needed for a specific task, such as next to a couch or alongside a bed.

Almost all fill lighting is created with portable table lamps or standing lamps. The great thing about lamps is that you can experiment to your heart's delight. Move a lamp to different areas and see how the light plays. Lighting plans are also organic in this way; if over time the light in a space doesn't suit you, it's easy to play around with fill lighting to achieve a better balance.

Ambient light, however, is just one part of the lighting equation. The second layer is more focused task lighting. Because you know where and how you work, this is an easier part of your lighting plan. It's just a matter of installing the right fixture for the job. For instance, almost any work desk benefits from a desk lamp, and the corner of the living room you've dedicated to a reading chair calls for a gooseneck or other downlighting fixture strong enough to make the words on the page show up clearly without straining the eyes.

The wealth of natural light in this eat-in kitchen is wisely supplemented with abundant artificial lighting from a sizable chandelier over the table and bright pendants over the island. Artificial lighting is even more essential in a room with so many dark, light-absorbing surfaces.

The recessed lights in this kitchen's ceiling provide abundant ambient light, while the pendants and hanging fixture over the table and sink add more specific lighting. All the fixtures are on dimmer switches.

Some rooms present fairly complex lighting challenges that call for a lot of thought. The kitchen is a prime example. There are usually several areas where food can be prepared, but only one or two where work is actually done. A kitchen lighting plan is an exercise in understanding your own preferences and positioning your task lighting accordingly.

The third layer is accent lighting. Accent lighting is meant to illuminate a specific feature in a room's design. It's really all about looking for where light isn't. Examples include picture lights that illuminate a specific piece of wall-hung art, interior lights for kitchen cabinets with glass fronts, and lights under the shelves in a bookshelf unit. Yes, it may seem like a part of a design you can easily do without, but accent lighting adds sophistication to a room and creates an upscale look. It makes for intriguing visual depth and enables you to highlight decorative and architectural features that might otherwise go unnoticed. Spend time thinking about the third layer; in most cases, it costs very little to institute a design feature with high impact.

> Getting interior design lighting just right is like walking a tightrope: Success is all about balance.

Determining what type of light you need and where you need it is the first and biggest part of your lighting puzzle. The next piece of that puzzle is selecting the actual fixtures that will provide just the right light, and the best look, for your design.

The right reading lamp—like the oversized adjustable floor lamp shown here—can turn any couch or chair into a comfy reading corner.

picking a fixture

Never lose sight of the fact that lighting fixtures are both decorative elements and functional appliances. Choosing the perfect fixture is part science and part design artistry. This much is certain, though; you could have a spectacular variety from which to choose. You'll find great examples of interesting lighting fixtures used in effective and innovative room designs in home design magazines. Clip the pages that catch your eye and add them to your Design Journal.

- Chandeliers. The classic hanging light fixture, chandeliers have been around since candles were the primary light source in homes. A chandelier is any hanging fixture that features multiple bulbs in separate arms. I divide the fixtures into two groups: traditional and everything else (sorry to be so technical!). Traditional chandeliers are metal—bronze, silver, iron—with a standard number of arms (four, six, eight) extending out from a central body. Non-traditional chandeliers can be made of just about any

A hot stove is no place to be fighting shadows and squinting to see what you're doing. That's why I always use lots of task lighting in the kitchen, usually including both under-hood and undercabinet fixtures. The fixtures over this cooktop are specially manufactured to hold up to heat and moisture.

material from plastic to wood, and often feature an irregular number of arms, with artsy forms that captivate the eye. These are, of course, regular features in dining rooms of any decor. I don't stop there. I see no reason not to use a chandelier as an unexpected decorative element in a bedroom or living room, as long as it's hung where nobody will bonk into it.

- Pendants. These hanging fixtures differ from chandeliers in that they are single lights suspended from a cord, a chain, or—less often—a fixed rod. That's a pretty basic definition that doesn't begin to do justice to the incredible array of pendant designs available. Pendants come small and large, subtle and outrageous. There really is a pendant style out there for everyone. Depending on the style you choose, pendants are perfect over a kitchen island, and a group of them can stand in for a chandelier over a dining room table. I think they even make great bedside lights that leave extra room on nightstands. One

Proving that there is a chandelier for any design style, this simple fixture dresses up a streamlined modern kitchen.

caveat: Be careful with pendants in which the bulb is exposed at all. The placement risks putting a glare right in someone's eyes.

- **Recessed.** These subtle fixtures are some of my favorites, and I'm not alone. The actual light fixture is hidden in the ceiling so that just the mounting lip and the bulb face show. Recessed fixtures are almost always equipped with halogen, xenon, or compact fluorescent bulbs that provide whiter, cooler, and crisper light than standard incandescents. Note: If you don't already have recessed features, installing them requires a lot of effort and expense, because you'll need to wire in new electrical boxes. However, if you have the budget or are planning a major remodel, recessed lighting can rock the look of a kitchen, bathroom, or bedroom. Whenever you go with new recessed fixtures, I'd strongly advise you to buy adjustable units so that you can direct the beams of light wherever you want them to go.

- **Tracks, rails, and cables.** Track or cable systems feature multiple heads that give you incredible lighting flexibility. Track lighting heads slide along in a ceiling-mounted channel that is hard-wired into an electrical box. The heads can be moved anywhere along the track's length and pointed in any direction. Sleek, minimal heads are the most popular, but traditional white "can" lights are still out there. Low-voltage "monorail" lights are a variation, with heads that slide along a rail suspended from the ceiling. The rails can be bent and cut to shapes from straight runs to S curves. The heads are lightweight and minimal, but I find that people go a bit wild with the rail, bending them in serpentine lines that don't necessarily put the lights where they are most needed and that can be a little distracting. The light from low-voltage lights is also weaker than from other fixtures. Cable systems have similar heads, which slide along low-voltage cables strung between two points. The

The unexpected can be design magic when done right. This hanging fixture, meant to mimic the look of a pillar candle chandelier, is just simple enough to fit into the restrained formal decor of this living room.

Recessed lighting is ideal for corridors, where hanging fixtures would be in the way. Arranged in a pattern for optimum light dispersal, these fixtures are equipped with halogen bulbs that produce a skin-tone-flattering bright white light.

heads appear to float, and it's a bit of a high-tech look. Any of these are great in a kitchen or other room as a way to fill out the ambient light or, in the case of smaller heads, highlight cabinetry, wall decoration, or art. It's adjustable and adaptable, yes, but the look doesn't fit smoothly with traditional, period or certain theme decors such as a country kitchen. They do, however, fit right into modern or contemporary decors. They also come in handy when a junction box is in an awkward corner of the room.

- **Sconces and wall-mounted fixtures.** Because they are mounted in the field of view, wall lights are as much a chance to snazz up a wall as they are sources of light. Always check that the wall lights you're considering look great turned on or off (most light stores and home centers mount them on a wall and show them lit at all times). These can be hardwired or, as is the case with some styles, plugged in. Of course, a cord hanging down from the fixture may not be your idea of a compelling visual, but it does open up the possibilities if you want a fixture that you can place anywhere in a room without much hassle. Before you buy the one that catches your eye, be sure you understand how the light from the fixture will play. Some sconces disperse light evenly in all directions, but many provide up-light, down-light, or both. Up-lighting and down-lighting can create drama, but they also create shadows. This much is for sure, though: Don't buy a wall fixture whose bulb is clearly visible through the shade—that's just asking for a glare spot in the middle of your design.

- **Table lamps.** Aside from the beauty of the form, the thing I like most about table lamps (and standing lamps, for that matter) is portability. They can easily be moved to where you need them—anywhere the cord can reach a wall outlet. There are so many types and styles that I can't begin to describe the variety, but let's just say that whatever size, shape, or finish you have in mind, it's out there somewhere. When I pick table lamps, I look for a shape that complements the other shapes in the space.

The wealth of pendant styles means that you can use them to make a real design statement while you add light sources. A row of stunning clear pendants adds to an eclectic look in this eat-in kitchen. The modern pendants work perfectly with the plain lines of the table and chairs and the bold colors of the carpet tiles.

- **Standing lamps.** The design flexibility that makes table lamps so popular applies to standing lamps as well. The bonus with this type of fixture is that it doesn't require a piece of furniture on which to sit. The most important choice you'll make in shopping for a standing lamp is head style. This gives incredible flexibility in redirecting light at a whim so that you can change from the perfect lighting for movie night to more dramatic illumination for a cocktail party. Like table lamps, standing lamps come in every style imaginable, so you should have no problem finding the one that suits the room perfectly and does everything you want it to do.
- **Specialty fixtures.** Specialty lighting fixtures are usually purpose-oriented and meant for a specific location, such as under-cabinet lighting for the kitchen. As often as not, the fixture itself is meant to be hidden. Buy these as the need arises for accent or task lighting.

shade specifics

Lampshades are, in my experience, some of the most overlooked decorative elements. Please don't assume that the shade the lamp is wearing when you buy it is the best possible shade for your design. Although some fixtures, such as ceiling and wall-mounted units, are specifically designed for one glass shade, many table and standing lights can be fitted with a number of hats.

You can pick from a variety of colors and patterns, or simpler, solid-color or beige shades. Bright-white shades tend to get dirty easily and can actually make the surrounding area look a little shabby. If I'm leaning in that direction, I'll buy a slightly off-white drum shade that enriches the light.

Keep in mind that depending on how densely colored the shade is, it will either be semi-opaque or it may tint the light that shines through. Lampshade shape is also a style indicator. Generally, a shade should not be taller than the lamp itself, and it should not permit the mount (known as a *harp*) or the bulb to show.

light bulb choices

Light bulbs are simple little things that can change the whole complexion of your interior design. The various types of light bulbs produce different colors of light:

- Incandescent bulbs are the most common and give off a warm, yellow light that's flattering to skin tones and interior design color.
- Halogens use far less energy to provide the same amount of light, but the light they produce is brighter and whiter than incandescent bulbs, and in some circumstances can seem a little harsh. The bulb itself gets very hot, so they can be risky to use below the ceiling line.
- Xenon bulbs produce a light colored somewhere between incandescents and halogens. They also stay cool.
- Fluorescents are energy-efficient, long-lasting bulbs that were, at one time, the ugly sister to all other types. Today's fluorescent bulbs produce a softer, more attractive light—most notably in compact fluorescent light (CFL) bulbs. Compact fluorescents can be used in any fixture that accommodates an incandescent bulb, and they are designed to produce light closer in color to an incandescent. Just be careful when handling or disposing of CFL bulbs; they contain mercury.
- LEDs (light-emitting diodes) are a chemically treated chip encased in a flexible housing.

Halogen spotlights are perfect accent lights to help bring attention to wall-mounted pieces such as the black-and-white prints that grace this bedroom. The rail lights can be adjusted to place light exactly where it's needed. This setup includes super-cool rail-mounted pendants that serve as bedside table lamps.

They are often used as purely decorative lights. They are small, adaptable, and easy and safe in just about any location, which makes them useful accent lights in some situations.

Lighting designers love to talk about light bulbs in terms of Kelvin temperatures. I don't know about you, but I don't walk around with a Kelvin meter in my back pocket. The quicker way to determine how nicely the light from a given bulb will make your interior colors look is to check the CRI (color rendering index) number on the package. The higher the number, the more realistic and accurate colors will look in the light from the bulb. A CRI of 70 or higher is most desirable in a home (parking lot lights are rated at 20; incandescent bulbs at 100).

lighting plans throughout the house

Every space in the house should have a thoughtful lighting plan. However, every room has its own needs and will call for a particular lighting strategy.

kitchen

Developing an interior design lighting plan is always a balancing act, but never more so than in a kitchen. The kitchen is a social center in today's home, which means lighting needs to create a pleasant mood, while accommodating food preparation, cooking, and eating. A common mistake is trying to use a single overhead light to illuminate all those different roles.

Yes, a strong, centralized ambient light source will be the cornerstone of your kitchen lighting plan, but it needs to be supplemented by several other types of lighting. It should also be adjustable (dimmer switches again!). If they work in your budget, recessed lights on a dimmer switch are a terrific way to fill out ambient light in the kitchen. Position them for maximum impact—the general rule is that they should be located along the front edge of counters, but think about positioning in an unconventional layout to follow traffic patterns, rather than just using the traditional grid. I also like to have a separate ambient light source over the table in an eat-in kitchen, which can be a ceiling fixture, pendant or even a strong set of rail lights.

Broad-range task lighting—fixtures that provide a level of light similar to an ambient source—is key in any kitchen. These include lighting over an island or workspace, and under all wall-mounted cabinets. Under-cabinet lighting comes in so many different varieties, including wired-in and plugged-in types, that there's just no reason not to include it. Here's a tip, though: People tend to place undercabinet fixtures toward the back of the cabinet. They are much more effective if mounted near the front of the cabinet so that they shine light where you actually do the work of preparing food.

The sink is another area where work light is essential. You need two sources of light, because if you use only a single overhead light, anybody working at the sink is likely to create a bothersome shadow over the basin. Accent lights fill out the kitchen lighting plan, and my favorites are interior lights for cabinets with glass fronts. Some people like to add cabinet-top or soffit lighting in the kitchen. In my view, this can easily look overdone, but use your own judgment. You can also help make the space safe for late-night snackers by running LED light cables along the kick spaces under cabinets.

Under-cabinet lights and stunning pendants combine to illuminate work surfaces and provide task lighting in a sleek kitchen.

Kitchens call for a mix of lighting. The stunning faux-marble laminate work surfaces and ebony cabinets in this space are well illuminated by the combination of recessed halogen lights, pendants, and hood lights—with a skylight providing abundant daytime ambient light.

bathroom

In contrast to the kitchen, a single overhead fixture can supply all the ambient light a modest bathroom requires. Recessed lights work well for a bathroom, as does a single, shaded overhead fixture. You rarely see track lighting used in the bathroom because the lights can create glare spots in the mirror and most track lights aren't moisture-proof. The strength of the ambient light is as important as the type of fixture you use. The light should be bright enough to see everything clearly, without being so bright as to be harsh. Task lighting is crucial in this space. The most important is the light around the mirror. Over-mirror fixtures are common, so it might seem a little surprising that I consider them enemies of effective bathroom lighting. Light shining down on your face creates deceptive shadows and makes putting on makeup or shaving more difficult.

The best bathroom mirror lighting involves two vertical fixtures, one on either side of the mirror. Of course, in some cases you simply don't have that option. If you have to go with an overhead light, I'd suggest using a long tubular fixture and bulb,

with a shade that disperses the light (or bath bar). You also need to make sure the tub or shower enclosure is adequately lit. This is as much a safety issue as anything else. Single bathroom-rated spotlights can light the space well. Finally, accent lights don't usually find a place in the bathroom, but that doesn't mean you have to follow that trend. A spot light that shows an interesting or unusual architectural feature in the bathroom can provide some visual interest to a room that is often—and justifiably—low key. You can also steal a page out of the kitchen lighting plan and run a strip of LED lights in the kick space under the vanity to make the bathroom easier to use in the middle of the night.

bedroom

Bedroom lighting is all about atmosphere. Rarely does a single overhead fixture suit the room and its lighting needs. I prefer a variety of light fixtures set at different heights around the room. I also use three-way lamps and bulbs where there is no dimmer; they are a way to maintain control over light that must accommodate very different activities in a short space of time (you can easily

Usually, the best way to light a bathroom is with a fixture on either side of the vanity. The light from these fixtures is softened by beige shades, creating an illumination that is flattering to skin tones.

add a dimmer to any plug-in light unless it's a CFL). Several portable fixtures produce a much softer blended lighting mix conducive to the calm and restful nature of most bedrooms. Lamps are key in creating ambient lighting throughout the room, and they also provide task lighting.

Once you've placed ambient lighting fixtures around the room, turn to the bed. Every bed deserves a light on either side, but the type of light should suit your lifestyle. Simple bed table lamps are fine for someone who usually goes to bed to go to sleep. But if you're a big reader, a wall-mounted, swing-arm lamp provides light just where you need, when you need it (make sure the bottom of the lampshade is in line with your chin when you're sitting up reading). Hanging pendant lights free up the top of nightstands, but they usually require that you get out of bed to turn them off. Lamps are ideal for a dressing table or small desk in the room; choose according to what you do there. A dressing table looks great flanked by two lamps, one on either side, especially if the dressing table is equipped with a mirror. A desk lamp is a better choice for a small desk used to pay bills and read important paperwork.

Don't forget more functional task lighting: Closets are much more usable when lit from within. Walk-in

or reach-in, you need a light in the closet. You can wire in a fixture or choose the simpler option of using battery-powered "puck" lights or other touch-activated fixtures. These are inexpensive, small, and easy to install.

living room and family room

These large common areas require more complicated lighting plans than most other rooms. An overhead fixture usually provides the primary ambient light, but many other fixtures and lighting types chime in to help these rooms fill the many roles they must play. The best living room or family room lighting is positioned in places that seem natural. They should also be easy to turn on or off to suit your mood, preferences, or activities.

I always start with the main seating area because this is where most people spend the bulk of their time. Generally, it's good to place a lamp on either side of a couch. This is an effective formula because people usually recline into a sofa corner to read, and one or both lamps can easily be turned off right from where you sit. However, this is not an unbreakable rule. I've actually seen—and loved—a high-ceilinged living room with a chandelier positioned high above the coffee table in the center of a grouping of chairs, a sofa, end tables, and a coffee table. It was just the right amount and type of light to create a welcoming social feel in the room.

When I put together a cozy corner for one of my clients, I always try to find a lamp with an adjustable head or neck.

Of course, a lot more than socializing goes on in these rooms. Often, people want to create a reading corner where they can relax and unwind with a good book or their favorite magazine. That begs a task light, and the best fixture is probably a standing light that can be adjusted to project a focused beam over an easy chair or divan. When I put together a cozy corner for one of my clients, I always try to find a lamp with an adjustable head or neck. That way, when nobody is using the corner, the lamp can be adjusted to fill in as needed for a party or as low lighting for TV viewing.

Enjoying a home theater setup, even if it is nothing more than a TV and cable box, means specialized task lighting. This is one area of the home that is regularly misunderstood and incorrectly lit. Viewing movies or TV shows in complete darkness is a recipe for eyestrain. On the other hand, too much ambient light washes out the picture on the screen and makes the viewing experience less enjoyable. The answer is to create very modest background light that prevents the eye from having to constantly adjust between total darkness and the flickering image on a screen. This means directing soft, weak light at the floor. It's often done with sconces or other types of down-lights positioned to the side and directed down behind the TV. Use other fixtures to softly down-light the room.

Lastly, living rooms and family rooms alike are prime candidates for the thoughtful use of accent lighting. Choose the fixture that best complements the art's frame without detracting from the art itself. Bookshelf lighting, positioned under shelves where the fixtures and bulbs are unseen, warms up a room and gives it a stately feel. Plug-in spotlights are really wonderful ways to highlight specific and stunning architectural features or statuary in a living room.

entryway

Entryway lighting, like all other entryway design elements, should ease the transition from outside to in while putting a welcoming face on the rest of the interior design. That's not rocket science, but it does take some thought. The lighting you need inside depends to a small degree on the doorway and exterior lighting. If your front door or sidelights are glass and your exterior lighting is bright, then the light entering the interior space

sabrina's rule

LIGHT TO RIGHT SIZE

Time and experience have taught us that there are certain heights and positioning that take best advantage of any given fixture:

- Kitchen and dining room tables should be at least 12 inches larger in diameter or width all around, than the width of a hanging fixture.
- Kitchen table pendants and chandeliers should hang about 30–34 inches above the table. A general rule is to add an inch for every additional foot of ceiling height above the standard 8 feet.
- Bathroom vanity mirror lights should be mounted on the sides of the mirror, preferably as close to 5 feet up from the floor as possible (this will suit most body heights). The lights should be around 30 inches apart, but no less than 24 inches. Where the mirror stretches across the wall, you may need to use over-mirror lights. Place these 74 inches or higher to accommodate tall people, and use shades on the lights—bare bulbs create harsh glare on skin.
- Pendants over a kitchen island should be 60–64 inches above the floor, which allows people a relatively unobstructed view across the room.
- Recessed lighting is generally most effective when placed at least 30 inches from a wall.
- Place pendants or semi-flush fixtures at least 36 inches above a pool table or Ping-Pong table.

after dark will diminish the need for strong ambient lighting. In any case, entryway lighting schemes are centered on a single overhead fixture. Smaller entryways need only a modest, flush-mount ceiling fixture. Larger entry halls, especially those with dramatic staircases off to one side, can support a more stylized lighting fixture—specifically a chandelier (although a vibrant, large pendant or set of pendants would work just as well). Size also determines whether I include a sconce or not. If the entryway is fairly large and cordoned off from the rest of the house by one or more walls, I like to use one or more sconces to provide fill lighting— corner shadows are the opposite of welcoming. As in a bathroom, I like to include a lamp on either side of the entryway mirror so that skin tones show to their best advantage in the mirror.

There are lots of ways to light a home office, but the lighting should always be responsive to the work and the layout of the space. This subtle work area in a wall of cabinets is distinctively lit with a small chandelier that adds a little unexpected panache to the room. Two halogen spotlights serve as both task and fill lighting, ensuring that there is an appropriate amount of light for working at the desk without eyestrain.

home office

A home office lighting plan revolves around functional task lighting, which usually equates to a simple overhead fixture or track light, a standing or table lamp in a corner of the room for fill lighting, and a good work lamp. I don't like to include a lot of accent lighting in a home office because it should be streamlined and neat. Where the home office has been carved out of a guest bedroom or one corner of a large living room, the lighting supplements the lighting plan for the larger area. In any case, a good desk lamp that works perfectly with the type of tasks you do (I always look for desk lamps with adjustable heads) is the key fixture. It should produce a light that is soft enough not to produce glare on a computer monitor, but strong enough to read clearly without straining your eyes.

dining room

Just as the dining room table is the centerpiece of the dining room, the over-table light is the center of the lighting plan in this social space. A chandelier is the traditional choice, but not just for traditional interiors. The amazing range of chandelier styles means that there's one

appropriate for any dining room, from Art Deco to modern. Any enclosed or partially enclosed dining room will need some fill lighting as well. I prefer to use a mix of uplight and downlight fixtures. Uplights add drama and make the room seem more exciting. Downlights help make for safe passage behind seated guests without tripping over rug edges or chair legs.. They are also out of the path of traffic and don't take up floor or tabletop space. Accent lights can add a little spice when used inside a glass-fronted hutch or china cabinet. You're usually storing some beautiful tableware there, and I think it's nice to show it off.

Get the light right in the room you are decorating, and all your efforts up to this point will come alive. The forms, colors, and textures in your design will show up just as you intended, and the lighting itself will reinforce the precise mood you captured in the mission statement you wrote at the beginning of this adventure. Now, all that's left is to put your signature on the design by choosing dynamic and personal accents.

Because there is often only one light fixture in a dining room, it presents the opportunity for a memorable design element. The one-of-a-kind chandelier over this round dining table is fitted with a drum shade that makes a vivid focal point out of an already eye-catching light source.

the eighth layer

accent your
interior design

I love to cook, which is why I always think of accents in terms of spices in a recipe; like spices, accents give a design a distinct flavor, making it unique and personal. However, the trick with both spices and accents is restraint (trust me—I've been there). You should be very thoughtful in choosing and placing decorative accents. As much as they can bring a design to life, they can also become distracting clutter when overused.

It's a problem that plagues many of the houses I visit—too many accents used in the wrong way or in the wrong places. We collect things over time. We take more and more pictures; we pick up pieces of art on vacations or buy that vase or photo frame that really speaks to us. The problem is, when you redesign a room, not all of those things will find a home. That's a hard fact to swallow sometimes, but if you want the most stylish decor that perfectly represents your own personal flair, it's a reality you'll have to accept. Some of your existing art, decorative items, candles, pillows, and other accents are simply not going to make the cut.

That's the tough part. The easier and more enjoyable piece of the puzzle is actually placing accents. They are, by their very nature, easy to move around, making them the simplest design elements to experiment with. If those vases don't work on the fireplace mantel, try your candlesticks and the terra cotta statuette there. When a piece of art simply isn't working on wall, take it down and try another. Trial and error is key to getting just the right mix of accents. It's also a really fun part of the design process, full of chances to be creative and the promise of instantaneous gratification. We might as well jump in, then, and start choosing your wall-mounted decorations.

wall-mounted art

I hereby bestow upon you the title of Curator. Like curators everywhere, you will use your exceptional judgment to select only the best pieces for your room design "show." That means that not every piece of art or photo you own necessarily gets put on display. Some simply won't work. Start by judging your art. Do the colors and patterns in the art conflict with the colors and patterns you've chosen for the space? This will be a lesser or greater factor depending on the size of the artwork. A small, 12-inch-×-14-inch print won't have as big an impact on your overall design as a painting measuring 6 feet × 4 feet.

Framing also influences what you can, should, and want to show. A modest, unadorned frame with a wide neutral mat isolates art or photography from the surrounding wall. A 2- to 4-inch mat is common these days, but you can go even wider to make the art stand on its own and avoid conflicts with surrounding colors or textures. Neutrals are the most common mat colors, because they provide a smooth visual transition from the background to the image itself. If your art is matted with a colored material, that color needs to work within the room's established color scheme. The same goes for the frame. Modest, simple outline frames work in most any room. The more intricate and stylized the frame, the more formal the room needs to be to support it. Keep this in mind: If an artwork or

Previous page: Candle displays don't need to fill a room to make their presence known. A grouping of elegant white pillar candles provides a small amount of fill lighting, but enriches the ambience of this bathroom in a big way. Glass containers add a touch of style to the vanity top as well.

photo you love looks off in the room, it may just need to be reframed to fit right into the design. You'd be surprised how just reframing a piece of art could completely change the look of it.

Once you've decided on exactly the art or photos you want to display, the next step is finding the perfect place to hang them. You can thank galleries and museums for a few basic guidelines that help you do just that. If you're hanging a single artwork, you want the center point of the image to be at eye level. People come in many different heights, so professionals use a baseline of 55–60 inches from the floor. I want to emphasize that this is where the center

sabrina's rule

PLAY THE ODD NUMBER

The eye finds odd numbers of objects intriguing and reads them as more exciting visuals than a group featuring even numbers. Unless you're purposefully using symmetry to create a calm, orderly environment, play around with three, five, or any other odd number of vases, decorative objects, or pictures on a wall.

Carefully chosen and positioned accents—including vases, bowls, and candles in glass candleholders—complement well-positioned wall art to personalize this living room without cluttering it.

An odd number of wall-mounted art pieces creates visual interest and are a great way to overcome the often bland feel of symmetry.

sabrina's rule

PAPER FIRST

Whether you're hanging a print in a bedroom, photos up a staircase, or a plate collection in a dining room, try out different positions to see which arrangement works best in the available wall space. Obviously, that could lead to a lot of nail holes, but there's a better way. I re-create the shapes I'm mounting with sheets of paper. I cut or tape sheets together as necessary to make exact copies of the shapes I want to hang. Then it's just a matter of taping them up until I find the right positions.

Always consider the background when hanging art. A single large photo works better than many smaller framed pieces would have against this wall with simple lines and basic white column. The image pops out at the viewer, just as any wall-mounted art or photo should.

of the artwork should hang, not the bottom edge (most people have a tendency to hang pictures and artwork too high or too low). This general rule also works for groupings: Center the dominant image or focal point of the grouping at the 60-inch mark. Which leads me to another bit of wisdom: If you're hanging photos or different-sized artwork in a line, align the centers along the 60-inch height.

Here's another helpful rule: A piece of art should never be more than 80 percent of the width of the piece of furniture underneath. (This rule works for framed mirrors as well!) In addition, a lot of designers feel that the bottom edge of the artwork should be between 8 inches and 10 inches above the furniture, but I usually focus on hanging the piece at eye level, even if that means positioning the bottom edge a bit higher.

Groupings of artwork or photos are even more of a challenge. Start with the centerpiece—the art or photo that should dominate the group (it's not necessarily the largest, just the strongest or most important to you). Position that one according to the 60-inch rule, and then design the rest of the layout branching out from that center point. Use a large area of open floor space or the paper trick described on the previous page. You'll get the most eye-pleasing design if you leave the same amount of space around each piece in the grouping, no matter how big or small. Grids are the easiest way to group wall-mounted decorations.

sabrina's

BEAUTIFUL, WISE PR

Custom prints may not be in you. get, but you can make your own very inexpensively. Find a set of frames at a thrift store, yard sale, or art store. Clean them up, prime them, paint them black, and finish them with a coat of clear acrylic. Then go online and search the black-and-white prints at the National Archives website (www. archives.gov/research/arc/). Pick some that you like and have them blown up at a local copy shop to fit the openings in the frames, and bang—a beautiful wall display for the price of couple of cappuccinos.

Grids are visually read as an overall shape—in this case, a wide rectangle. Not only does the shape of this grid echo the width of the bed, the matting complements the trim on the window treatments, and the frames and photos themselves pick up the colors of the bedding, tying the look together.

ecorative accents are
your chance
to personalize
your design.

Regardless of the pattern you choose, I can't stress enough that you should spend time playing around with the arrangement. Even accomplished graphic designers will try out many different configurations when laying out different shapes. Experiment and trust your eye, because the fact is that certain arrangements are pleasing to the eye. When you find the right one for your particular grouping, you'll know it.

One last word on art and photo groupings: There is another decorative element that can change the perception of a space, much like stripes do. If a series of framed works is set in a horizontal line, the room will seem more expansive. If the arrangement is strongly vertical in nature, the ceiling will seem higher.

These general guidelines hold true no matter what you're mounting on the wall. A collection of plates will follow the same basic logic. However, sometimes you will have to bend the rules a bit. For instance, hanging a full-scale tapestry on a wall may mean that there is no way to position the visual center 60 inches above the floor. In a case like that, back up, and view the wall as a matted frame, positioning overlarge art in the most attractive position between floor and ceiling.

Here's a cool way to mount art and make it functional at the same time. This painting has been hung (with the center almost exactly at 60 inches) on rollers from a stainless steel track—a system normally used for doors. But here, the art conceals the TV except for when it comes time for a movie. Neat, sleek, and totally fitting for the modern living room style.

Right: An assortment of glass vases and containers provide accents in contrast to the solidity of the comfortable furnishings in this seaside house. The glass colors echo the room's color scheme, and the sprinkling of seashells brings the exterior environment into the decor.

mirror, mirror, on the wall

Mirrors are some of the most interesting and dynamic wall-mounted accents. Start with the shape of the frame. Rectangles or squares are a conventional look, but circular mirrors can be fun and lively, if a bit more informal in style. The frames can be used to complement existing textures, lines, or colors in the design, or you can pick those that stand out all on their own, like a gold-painted starburst.

Position mirrors according to the same rules you would use for wall-mounted art or photos, but keep them out of the path of direct light sources to avoid glare spots. Positioning can also be affected by function. As decorative as a mirror may be, it always brightens a space and creates a more open feel in a room. However, one word of caution: Too many mirrors on the same wall, or mirrors use[] each other, can create confusing and di[] visual imagery. I tend to use restraint an[] mirrors on only one wall of a room I'm de[]

adornable tabletops and shelves

Displaying objects of any sort on a table or shelf is all about maintaining visual balance. Accessorize with odd numbers to create the most visual interest. Use pops of colors (maybe even one object of an odd bold color for interest). Try not to use accessories smaller than a grapefruit (too many create clutter). A squat, round vase has more perceived mass than a long, thin candlestick. Three candlesticks, though, may well have the same perceived mass as a squat, round vase.

I'm pretty sure you wouldn't buy a plastic sofa. I feel safe saying that plastic kitchen cabinets aren't going to be your first choice. So why default to cheap-looking plastic nursery pots that the plants come in from the garden center? Given that you'll be introducing a modest number of plants into your room design, give them a worthwhile home. Nice plant pots won't break the bank. Find a lacquered pot that complements your color scheme, or opt for a terra cotta, stone, or other natural material that will fit into almost any decor. You can even replant them in high-quality, well-designed plastic pots. Whatever containers you choose, I suggest keeping all the plants in a room in similar or complementary pots to maintain visual continuity. You can even use potted plants as design continuity markers from one room to another.

I always advise my clients to consider the viewer. Organize tabletop or shelf displays according to how and where they are most likely to be viewed. I build the composition from front to back. Basic rules will guide you: small objects in front, larger objects in back. Don't block the view of any object in the composition or it doesn't need to be there.

Most of the time, collections scream "clutter!" One in the house (like model cars in a child's room) is okay, but a Coca-Cola collection in the living room is unacceptable.

the *living* room

I like to think of accessorizing a room as an organic process, one that can evolve over time and allows for change. That's why plants are such great accents: They change all on their own. Not to mention that a living, growing decoration gives a room a great vibe and can even improve indoor air quality.

When it comes to using plants in a room, I go bold or go subtle. I don't like to get stuck in between. A room divider of tall evergreens or a vertical garden? Bold. A small Boston fern or peace lily in a lacquered pot? Subtle. No matter which way you go, though, the keys to successfully incorporating plants as decoration are picking the right plant and choosing scintillating containers.

Only certain plants will grow well in the confines of your home. You can find most of the common varieties at local nurseries or large home centers. Most are foliage plants, offering versions of green and white. Pay attention to the form of the plant—some sprawl, some grow compactly, and some spike upward. Look for a growth habit that complements the other forms in your design.

> *When grouping houseplants, I rarely use more than three unless the plant is large.*

A miniature herb garden will perk up a kitchen, but mostly I prefer to use standard foliage houseplants because they are low maintenance and easy to design around. When grouping houseplants, I rarely use more than three unless the plant is large (say, a ficus tree). A single small plant can look a little bit like an orphan, but when you start clustering more than three, you risk things looking a little like a jungle and drawing attention away from other design elements.

accessorizing with candles

Candles have the power to infuse an interior with a sense of hominess and warmth. They are also

An artfully arranged collection of antique clocks adds a distinctive design element to this low-key home office. The clocks reinforce the homey style, that is further complemented by an embroidered throw pillow and three antique machinery pieces on the top of the cabinet unit.

inexpensive, and there are so many shapes and styles that you can easily find the perfect candles to accent your specific design.

Taper candles are the most traditional style and their long thin shapes are indisputably elegant. They are the candle of choice for most dining rooms, and the candleholders they require come in so many styles that are themselves stunning accents. Formal dining rooms are best served by candelabras, although I prefer to place them on sideboards or other surfaces rather than in the middle of the table, where they can block the view between diners sitting across from each other. You can also find wall-mounted sconce-type candleholders for tapers, which can be a stunning addition to dining rooms. Tapers come in many different colors, but I prefer white or neutral tones

Exposed shelving in a bathroom full of special treats for guests can be a wonderfully colorful place for accents.

to let the shape and flame dominate. Always buy dripless tapers to make your life easier, and always use unscented, dripless candles in a dining space.

Pillar candles are a wildly popular style. Shaped like miniature columns, they come in many different diameters, heights, colors, and styles of wax; some are even decorated with words, charms, symbols, or stencils. Although a hefty pillar candle can hold its own in any room, I love to combine several different pillars. Use colored versions to create little pockets of vibrant accents. However, a grouping of standard off-white pillars several different heights and diameters is the most sophisticated look. This type of cluster can liven up any room, as a coffee table centerpiece, a dresser decoration, or a kitchen table accent. Pillars can even stand in for tapers on a dining room table. They are long-burning and just plain lovely.

> A single votive can be an interesting and unexpected visual, but groups of votives have a certain magic about them when all the candles are lit.

Votive candles are a more modest cousin to the taper. They are generally made in a standard height of around 2 inches to fit in a votive holder. Because they melt completely, they should always be displayed and used in a holder. Votive candles come in many different colors, but white or yellow are the most classic and the most adaptable. There are so many ways to incorporate votives as decorative accents it's hard to know where to begin. A single votive can be an interesting and unexpected visual, but groups of votives have a certain magic about them when all the candles are lit. They are great indoors and out, and I like to sprinkle them around a room, to create little points of flame that add spice to a cocktail party or any special get-together.

Tea lights are the baby sister to votives. They are almost flat candles that are usually dropped into special candleholders with shallow cavities. To me, these are elegant small accents, but the candles burn down very quickly and I almost prefer the wide range of artsy tea light candleholders more than the candles themselves. I find the candles are most engaging when used outside for cocktail parties and poolside celebrations.

Container candles come in every style imaginable, because the wax is poured into the container. Cups, vases, mugs, and custom-made containers can all hold candles. I use these on a case-by-case basis; if I come across a candle in a compelling container, I'll use it to accent a design just as I would use a tabletop accent. The big advantage is that container candles burn for a long time, and the wax is contained—so there's no cleanup.

I know you're smarter than this, but I'd be remiss if I didn't mention that you should never group candles, or place individual candles, near flammable materials, such as window treatments. You should also be careful about dripping wax, which can ruin rugs, carpets, and many furniture finishes.

pillow perfect

Throw pillows are a great way to soften the hard edges in your design, while adding splashes of color, texture, and a sense of fun and comfort. All of this makes pillows a high-impact accent in any design. Pillow sizes and shapes vary greatly, creating even more potential variety.

- **Knife.** Named for the skinny edges that resemble knife edges, these are the most common throw pillows and work with every style of decor—from super formal to super casual. What I love about them is that they come in several different standardized sizes that you can choose from according to where you're using the pillow. More importantly, they come in every fabric under the sun and range from simple solid colors

A scattering of throw pillows introduces stripes into the room design, and ties the sofas and chair together by mirroring the color of the opposing furniture. The pillows add a welcoming appeal, while tabletop sculptures introduce personal touches of style.

to totally off-the-wall patterns. Mix and match these pillows on a couch, or use one really vibrant one to accent an easy chair.

- Floor. Also called floor cushions, these are throw pillows for casual sitting (or lying). Many are like oversized knife pillows, available in the same variety of fabrics and looks. However, many floor pillows are unique designs—such as cubes that attach to one another with magnetic fasteners—that can make watching TV, having a small party or just lounging a fun and supremely comfy experience. No matter what style you choose, you should have the floor space to accommodate the pillows and still leave pathways for foot traffic through the room. The style and lounge-ability of floor pillows is a casual look that is not appropriate for formal, period style, or traditional rooms. In a family room, a contemporary interior, or even a modern decor, floor pillows can be an

interesting and relaxing way to add seating and accents with one bold stroke.

- Box. These pillows look like furniture cushions; rather than the closed edge of a knife pillow, they have wide edges, usually with piping. You'll find box pillows in a more limited range of fabrics and designs than other pillow styles because box pillows are not as popular. They are a distinctive style that is best suited for more formal couches and chairs. The squared-off look just doesn't complement a wide range of furniture. More often, larger versions are used as floor cushions.

- Bolster. Another classic, bolster pillows look like a sausage with both ends cut off. They add variation in shape, along with the same selection of fabrics and designs you'd find among knife pillows. Bolsters are used everywhere, but they tend to look their best when paired with furniture that has a squared-off shape, and on

Knife

Floor

Box

Bolster

beds, as an accent to more traditional pillows. Bolsters can also be useful if you use the couch for reclining—they fit neatly under your neck while you're watching TV.

You can be a little extravagant in choosing throw and other decorative pillows. Here's what I suggest you look for:

- Texture and material contrasts. Select throw pillows in a different fabric than the couch, sofa, or other area where they will be placed, to help them stand out and to take advantage of naturally scintillating choices such as raw silk.
- Pops of color and pattern. The small size of most throw pillows means a bold color or pattern won't overwhelm the design. Even if you incorporated other patterns into your design,

don't be afraid to buy patterned throw pillows. In general, if you've gone with subtle patterns in wallpaper, window treatments, and/or rugs, choose a bolder pattern for the pillows—and vice versa.

- The main color in the throw pillow should complement your color scheme.

Set your accents in place, and you've essentially put jewelry on the outfit of your interior design. You've worked your way through several layers, and the one last thing you need to do is go back to your notes, check your mission statement (see the "Mission: Possible!" section in *The First Layer: Understand Your Space and Plan Your Design*), and look at the design through the lens of your intentions. If it's not quite there, make adjustments.

Get all the elements in the right place, and the room will come together as beautifully as this one did. When your room is undeniably stylish and completely comfortable, you'll know you're finished.

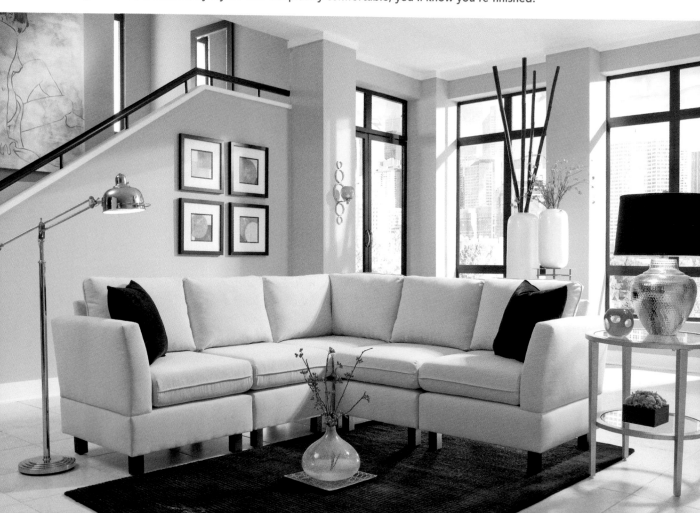

a never-ending adventure

I hope it's clear that the layering process is an organic one, in that it can change and adapt to suit anybody's needs and tastes. (I also hope you've had fun in the process, because that's a key part of it!) That organic nature is open-ended; in a sense, your design is never finished.

I mean that in a good way. If you've developed each layer carefully and given due thought to your style and free rein to your creativity, you're looking at your dream design. However, lives go on, people change, your tastes evolve, and your interior design should evolve as well. It pays to revisit the layers from time to time to check in on your design. That's why I give my clients the Design Journal I've developed for them and ask them to keep it. It's a great baseline against which they can judge new decorations, including holiday and special-occasion decorating. When your Design Journal begins to seem out of touch with your life and your tastes, it's time to start the adventure anew.

In the meantime, look at your design as a living, breathing thing with the design journal as your guide. Swap out furnishings that become outdated or timeworn with newer pieces according to the original ideas you had about a room's layout. Adjust your lighting plan to make a space even more usable, comfortable, and enjoyable. Change textiles, art, and tabletop decorations regularly to refresh your design—but follow the same logic you used in the first place.

For now, though, take a breath and pat yourself on the back for a job well done. Then call your friends. It's time to have a party and show off your fabulous new design!

Photo Credits

Page iv: (top) see page 39; (middle) see page 45; (bottom) see page 171

Page v: see page 124

Page vi: Photo @ Tim Coburn

introduction

Page 2: (top) Photo courtesy of Century Furniture, www.centuryfurniture.com, (800) 852-5552. CENTURY is a registered trademark owned by Century Furniture LLC; (bottom) Photo courtesy of Bertch Cabinet Manufacturing, Inc., www.bertch.com

Page 3: Photo courtesy of Bertch Cabinet Manufacturing, Inc., www.bertch.com

Page 4: Photo © Rodenberg - Fotolia.com

the first layer: understand your space and plan your design

Page 5: Photo courtesy of DuroDesign Flooring, Inc., www.duro-design.com, (888) 528-8518

Page 7: (top) Photo by Lucky Photo / Shutterstock.com; (bottom) Photo by Chris Rodenberg Photography / Shutterstock.com

Page 9: Photo courtesy of Mohawk Flooring, www.mohawkflooring.com, (800) 266-4295

Page 10: Photo courtesy of Crystorama Lighting, www.crystorama.com, (516) 931-9090

Page 11: ©iStockphoto.com/Poligonchik

Page 13: Photo © Larry Malvin / Stocklib.com

Page 14: Photo courtesy of Trend Lighting

Page 15: Photo courtesy of BEHR Process Corporation, www.behr.com, (877) 237-6158

the second layer: choose your colors

Page 17: Photo courtesy of Pratt & Lambert Paints, www.prattandlambert.com, (800) 289-7728

Page 19: Photo © Patrick Barta / Cornerhousestock.com

Page 21: (top) Photo courtesy of Forbo Flooring, www.forboflooringna.com, (800) 842-7839; (bottom) Photo courtesy of Bertch Cabinet Manufacturing, Inc., www.bertch.com

Page 22: Photo by Anthony Berenyi / Shutterstock.com

Page 23: Photo © Jeff Green / Cornerhousestock.com

Page 24: Photo courtesy of BEHR Process Corporation, www.behr.com, (877) 237-6158

Page 25: Photo by Stephen Coburn / Shutterstock.com

Page 26: Photo courtesy of Simplicity Sofa, www.simplicitysofas.com, (800) 813-2889

Page 27: (top) Photo courtesy of McGuire, www.mcguirefurniture.com, (800) 662-4847; (bottom) Photo © Morris Gindi / Cornerhousestock.com

Page 28: Photo by Chris Rodenberg Photography / Shutterstock.com

Page 29: Photo courtesy of Armstrong, www.armstrong.com, (800) 233-3823

Page 30: (top) Photo by Rade Kovac / Shutterstock.com; (bottom) Photo courtesy of Flor, Inc., www.flor.com, (866) 281-3567

Page 33: (top) Photo courtesy of BEHR Process Corporation, www.behr.com, (877) 237-6158; (bottom) Photo courtesy of Crystorama Lighting, www.crystorama.com, (516) 931-9090

Page 34: Photo courtesy of Bertch Cabinet Manufacturing, Inc., www.bertch.com

Page 35: Photo courtesy of Wood-Mode, Inc., www.wood-mode.com, (877) 635-750

Page 36: Photo by Pics721 / Shutterstock.com

Page 37: Photo by Chris Rodenberg Photography / Shutterstock.com

Page 38: Photo © Jessie Walker / Cornerhousestock.com

Page 39: Photo courtesy of Ballard Designs, www.ballarddesigns.com, (800) 536-7551

Page 41: (top) Photo © Ken Rice / Cornerhousestock.com; (bottom) Photo © Jamie Salomon / Cornerhousestock.com

Page 42: Photo by Cora Reed / Shutterstock.com

the third layer: select your surface treatments

Page 43: Photo courtesy of Forbo Flooring, www.forboflooringna.com, (800) 842-7839

Page 45: (top) Photo courtesy of Armstrong, www.armstrong.com, (800) 233-3823; (bottom) Photo courtesy of Tendances Concept; kitchen design: Tendances Concept; glass countertop: ThinkGlass

Page 46: Photo ©iStockphoto.com/Phototropic

Page 47: Photo by Yampi / Shutterstock.com

Page 48: Photo courtesy of Mohawk Flooring, www.mohawkflooring.com, (800) 266-4295

Page 49: (top) Photo courtesy of Armstrong, www.armstrong.com, (800) 233-3823; (bottom left) Photo courtesy of Mohawk Flooring, www.mohawkflooring.com, (800) 266-4295; (bottom right) Photo courtesy of Mountain Lumber Company, www.mountainlumber.com, (800) 445-2671

Page 50: Photo courtesy of Mountain Lumber Company, www.mountainlumber.com, (800) 445-2671

Page 51: Photos courtesy of Pioneer Millworks, pioneermillworks.com, (800) 951-9663

Page 52: (first column) Photos courtesy of Pioneer Millworks, www.pioneermillworks.com, (800) 951-9663; (second column) Photo by Yampi / Shutterstock.com

Page 53: Photo by Chris Rodenberg Photography / Shutterstock.com

Page 54: (top) Photo courtesy of Artistic Tile, www.artistictile.com, (877) 528-5401; (bottom) Photo by Lucky Photo / Shutterstock.com

Page 55: Photo courtesy of Mohawk Flooring, www.mohawkflooring.com, (800) 266-4295

Page 56: Photo courtesy of Armstrong, www.armstrong.com, (800) 233-3823

Page 57: Photo courtesy The Craft-Art Company, Inc., www.craft-art.com, (404) 352-5625

Page 58: Photo courtesy of Mohawk Flooring, www.mohawkflooring.com, (800) 266-4295

Page 59: Photo courtesy of Mohawk Flooring, www.mohawkflooring.com, (800) 266-4295

Page 60: Photo courtesy of Mohawk Flooring, www.mohawkflooring.com, (800) 266-4295

Page 61: Photo courtesy of Flor, Inc., www.flor.com, (866) 281-3567

Page 62: Photo courtesy of Mohawk Flooring, www.mohawkflooring.com, (800) 266-4295

Page 63: Photo courtesy of Bertch Cabinet Manufacturing, Inc., www.bertch.com

Page 64: Photo courtesy of The House of Smiths, www.thehouseofsmiths.com

Page 65: Photo courtesy of Century Furniture, www.centuryfurniture.com, (800) 852-5552

Pages 66: Photos by Raef Grohne, www.Architectural Photographer.com / StockPhotosofHomes.com

Page 68: Photo courtesy of BEHR Process Corporation, www.behr.com, (877) 237-6158

Page 69: Photo courtesy of Bertch Cabinet Manufacturing, Inc., www.bertch.com

Page 70: Photo by Pics721 / Shutterstock.com

Page 71: (top) Photo courtesy of Armstrong, www.armstrong.com, (800) 233-3823; (bottom) Photo courtesy of Artistic Tile, www.artistictile.com, (877) 528-5401

Page 72: Photos courtesy of Diamond Tech Tile, www.dttiles.com, (800) 937-9593

Page 73: Photo by Chris Rodenberg Photography / Shutterstock.com

Page 74: (top) Photo courtesy of Diamond Tech Tile, www.dttiles.com, (800) 937-959; (bottom) Photo courtesy of Cambria, www.CambriaUSA.com, (866) CAMBRIA

Page 75: Photo courtesy of Granite Transformations, www.granitetransformations.com

Page 76: Photos courtesy of CaesarStone, www.caesarstoneus.com, (818) 779-0999

Page 77: Photo ©iStockphoto.com/Springboard, Inc.

Page 78: (top) Photo courtesy of Formica Corporation, www.formica.com, (800) FORMICA; (bottom) Photo courtesy The Craft-Art Company, Inc., www.craft-art.com, (404) 352-5625

Page 79: Photo courtesy The Craft-Art Company, Inc., www.craft-art.com, (404) 352-5625

Page 80: (top) Photo courtesy of Formica Corporation, www.formica.com, (800) FORMICA; (bottom) Photo courtesy of Plain & Fancy Custom Cabinetry, plainfancycabinetry.com, (800) 447-9006

the fourth layer: integrate storage to organize your space

Page 81: Photo courtesy of BEHR Process Corporation, www.behr.com, (877) 237-6158

Page 83: (top) Photo courtesy of Bertch Cabinet Manufacturing, Inc., www.bertch.com; (bottom) Made in Italy by Clei. Photo courtesy of Resource Furniture, www.resourcefurniture.com, (212) 753-2039

Page 84: Photo courtesy of ClosetMaid, www.closetmaid.com, (800) 874-0008

Page 85: Photo courtesy of ClosetMaid, www.closetmaid.com, (800) 874-0008

Page 87: Photo courtesy of Bertch Cabinet Manufacturing, Inc., www.bertch.com

Page 88: (top) Photo courtesy of ClosetMaid, www.closetmaid.com, (800) 874-0008; (bottom) Photo courtesy of California Closets, www.californiaclosets.com, (888) 336-9707

Page 89: Photos courtesy of ClosetMaid, www.closetmaid.com, (800) 874-0008

Page 90: (top) Photo courtesy of Crystorama Lighting, www.crystorama.com, (516) 931-9090; (bottom) Photo by Chris Rodenberg Photography / Shutterstock.com

Page 91: (top) Photo courtesy of ClosetMaid, www.closetmaid.com, (800) 874-0008; (bottom) Page 91: Photo courtesy of Rakks, www.rakks.com, (800) 826-6006

Page 92: Photo courtesy of CaesarStone, www.caesarstoneus.com, (818) 779-0999

Page 93: (top) Photo courtesy of The Container Store, www.containerstore.com, (888) 266-8246; (bottom) Photo courtesy of CaesarStone, www.caesarstoneus.com, (818) 779-0999

Page 95: Photo courtesy of Marvin Windows and Doors, www.marvin.com, (888) 537-7828

Page 96: Photo courtesy of ClosetMaid, www.closetmaid.com, (800) 874-0008

Page 98: Photo courtesy of McGuire, www.mcguirefurniture.com, (800) 662-4847

Page 99: Photo courtesy of Solid Wood Closets, www.SolidWoodClosets.com, (800) 351-9144

Page 100: (top) Photo courtesy of Wood-Mode, Inc., www.wood-mode.com, (877) 635-7500; (bottom left and right) Photos courtesy of ClosetMaid, www.closetmaid.com, (800) 874-0008

Pages 101–103: Photos courtesy of ClosetMaid, www.closetmaid.com, (800) 874-0008

Page 104: Photo courtesy of California Closets, www.californiaclosets.com, (888) 336.9707

the fifth layer: edit your furniture

Page 105: Photo ©iStockphoto.com/Terry J Alcorn, Inc.

Page 107: (top) Photo ©iStockphoto.com/Terry J Alcorn, Inc.; (bottom) Photo courtesy of Crystorama Lighting, www.crystorama.com, (516) 931-9090

Page 108: (top) Photo by Chris Rodenberg Photography / Shutterstock.com; (bottom) Made in Italy by Clei. Photo courtesy of Resource Furniture, www.resourcefurniture.com, (212) 753-2039

Page 109: Photo courtesy of Mohawk Flooring, www.mohawkflooring.com, (800) 266-4295

Page 110: Photo © Larry Malvin / Stocklib.com

Page 111: Photo courtesy of Cambria, www.CambriaUSA.com, (866) CAMBRIA

Page 112: Photo © Rodenberg - Fotolia.com

Page 113: Photo courtesy of Danze, Inc. (Tom Connors, photographer) www.danze.com, (877) 530-3344

Page 114: (top) Photo courtesy of The Joinery, www.thejoinery.com, (800) 259-6762; (bottom) Photo by Pics721 / Shutterstock.com

Page 115: Photo by Hadrian / Shutterstock.com

Page 116: Photo courtesy of Century Furniture, www.centuryfurniture.com, (800) 852-5552

Page 117: Photo courtesy of California Closets, www.californiaclosets.com, (888) 336-9707

Page 118: Photo courtesy of Ballard Designs, www.ballarddesigns.com, (800) 536-7551

Page 120: Photo courtesy of ClosetMaid, www.closetmaid.com, (800) 874-0008

Page 121: Photo by Pics721 / Shutterstock.com

Page 122: (top) Photo by Chris Rodenberg Photography / Shutterstock.com; (bottom) Photo courtesy of Marvin Windows and Doors, www.marvin.com, (888) 537-7828

Page 123: Photo courtesy of Granite Transformations, www.granitetransformations.com

Page 124: (top) Photo courtesy of Crystorama Lighting, www.crystorama.com, (516) 931-9090; (bottom) Photo courtesy of Wood-Mode, Inc., www.wood-mode.com, (877) 635-7500

Page 125: (top) Photo courtesy of Cambria, www.CambriaUSA.com, (866) CAMBRIA; (bottom) Photo courtesy The Craft-Art Company, Inc., www.craft-art.com, (404) 352-5625

Page 126: Photo courtesy of Resource Furniture, www.resourcefurniture.com, (212) 753-2039

Page 127: Photo courtesy of Baker, www.bakerfurniture.com, (800) 592-2537

Page 128: Photo by Chris Rodenberg Photography / Shutterstock.com

Page 129: Photo courtesy of ClosetMaid, www.closetmaid.com, (800) 874-0008

Page 130: Made in Italy by Clei. Photo courtesy of Resource Furniture, www.resourcefurniture.com, (212) 753-2039

the sixth layer: select your textiles

Page 131: Photo courtesy of Thibaut Inc., www.thibautdesign.com, (800) 223-0704

Page 133: Photo courtesy of Century Furniture, www.centuryfurniture.com, (800) 852-5552

Page 135: Photo courtesy of Baker, www.bakerfurniture.com, (800) 592-2537

Page 136: Photo courtesy of Marvin Windows and Doors, www.marvin.com, (888) 537-7828

Page 137: Photo by Tr1sha / Shutterstock.com

Page 138: Photo by Chris Rodenberg Photography / Shutterstock.com

Page 139: Photo courtesy of Smith+Noble, LLC.

Page 141: (top) Photo by Chris Rodenberg Photography / Shutterstock.com; (bottom) Photo courtesy of Pratt & Lambert Paints, www.prattandlambert.com, (800) 289-7728

Page 142: Photo courtesy of Pratt & Lambert Paints, www.prattandlambert.com, (800) 289-7728

Page 145: Photo ©iStockphoto.com/Contrastaddict

Page 146: Photo courtesy of Crystorama Lighting, www.crystorama.com, (516) 931-9090

Page 147: Photo courtesy of Capel Rugs, www.capelrugs.com, (800) 382-6574

Page 149: Photo ©iStockphoto.com/Poligonchik

Page 150: (top) Photo courtesy of Marvin Windows and Doors, www.marvin.com, (888) 537-7828; (bottom) Photo courtesy of Kallista, www.kallista.com, (888) 452-5547

the seventh layer: illuminate your design

Page 151: Photo © Chipper Hatter / Cornerhousestock.com

Page 153: Photo © George Mayer - Fotolia.com

Page 154: Photo by Chris Rodenberg Photography / Shutterstock.com

Page 155: Photo by Pics721 / Shutterstock.com

Page 156: Photo by Sklep Spozywczy / Shutterstock.com

Page 157: (top) Photo by John Wollwerth / Shutterstock.com; (bottom) Photo by Sklep Spozywczy / Shutterstock.com

Page 158: Photo by Chris Rodenberg Photography / Shutterstock.com

Page 159: Photo by Gorin / Shutterstock.com

Page 160: Photo courtesy of Flor, Inc., www.flor.com, (866) 281-3567

Page 161: Photo courtesy of Encompass Lighting Group, www.encompasslighting.com, (847) 410-4400

Page 162: Photo courtesy of Wood-Mode, Inc., www.wood-mode.com, (877) 635-7500

Page 163: Photo courtesy of Formica Corporation, www.formica.com, (800) FORMICA

Page 164: Photo by Tr1sha / Shutterstock.com

Page 166: (top) Photo courtesy of ClosetMaid, www.closetmaid.com, (800) 874-0008; (bottom) Photo courtesy of Crystorama Lighting, www.crystorama.com, (516) 931-9090

the eighth layer: accent your interior design

Page 167: Photo courtesy of Encompass Lighting Group, www.encompasslighting.com, (847) 410-4400

Page 169: Copyright © 2009, www.GeorgeGutenberg.com

Page 170: (top) Photo © Jessie Walker / Cornerhousestock.com; (bottom) Photo courtesy of McGuire, www.mcguirefurniture.com, (800) 662-4847

Page 171: Photo courtesy of Pratt & Lambert Paints, www.prattandlambert.com, (800) 289-7728

Page 172: Photo courtesy of Krown Lab, www.krownlab.com, (503) 292-6998

Page 173: Photo courtesy of Pratt & Lambert Paints, www.prattandlambert.com, (800) 289-7728

Page 175: Photos courtesy of ClosetMaid, www.closetmaid.com, (800) 874-0008

Page 177: Photo by Chris Rodenberg Photography / Shutterstock.com

Page 178: Photo courtesy of Simplicity Sofa, www.simplicitysofas.com, (800) 813-2889

index